Advance Praise for Living in Expectancy

Living in Expectancy is a compelling story of one woman's journey of faith. From a seemingly tragic accident that brought the end of youthful dreams, to accounts of multiplied answers to prayer throughout her life and the lives of her family, Cindy Wenger captivatingly tells of her growing and dynamic intimate relationship with God and of her deepening personal experience with the gifts of the Holy Spirit. The story of God's faithfulness will deeply challenge and uplift any reader.

Read it with an open mind and heart and in expectancy and thankfulness for the life God has yet ahead for you.

—Dr. Jack Schwarz, retired chair of the Biola
University Department of Music and dean emeritus,
the Division of Fine Arts and Communication

My wife and I first met Cindy and her husband, Mike, when they moved to Redding. From the beginning, she impressed me as a woman of peace and faith. After reading her story, I have come to understand even better where her peace comes from. Cindy has discovered the secret of facing life with hope, joy, and the realization that Jesus' love is greater than her situation. *Living in Expectancy* unfolds how her life's unexpected tragedies lead her time and time again to put her faith in Jesus. Cindy's walk of faith is a journey to a greater intimacy with the Lord. Through her story you will see firsthand that trusting God is always your best option and choosing hope and joy is choosing strength to face the impossible. This book is more than a testimony of healing. It is an example of living life with a kingdom mindset, and it provides insights into how to stand on the promises of God.

—H. Don Mayer, principal, Bethel Christian
School, Redding, California

Cindy Wenger has penned a powerful story of faith beating the odds. Personal vignettes draw the reader into sunny days following tragedy and hope on the journey. Fellow strugglers are welcomed here and handed courage to continue the pursuit.

—Terry and Mary Inman, pastors of Harbor
Light Church, Fremont, California

Even before we finished Cindy's book *Living in Expectancy,* my wife and I discovered that we were already putting into practice a renewed "expectancy" and a fresh, faith-filled attitude toward God. This book brought us straight back to our first love and how we encountered the Lord's great and faithful promises as young parents. How great it seemed to trust God at every step, praise Him for everything and every situation that came our way. Now, while we are in our fifties, Cindy brought us back into His presence with expectancy again. Whether you're a brand-new Believer or a well-seasoned, mature Christian, this book offers to you the same "newness" feeling of renewed life in Christ. Her stories will simply build your faith. It's inescapable. We both heartily recommend this book to all readers who wish to walk more closely in faith with their Savior.

—Steve and Derene Shultz, cofounders of The Elijah
List and author of *Can't You Talk Louder, God?*

Living in Expectancy

When You Feel Like Giving Up

Cindy Wenger

WESTBOW·
PRESS
A DIVISION OF THOMAS NELSON
& ZONDERVAN

Scripture quotations are from the New King James Version. Copyright ©1982 by Thomas Nelson, Inc. Used by permission. All rights reserved.

Scripture quotations taken from the New American Standard Bible®, Copyright © 1960, 1962, 1963, 1968, 1971, 1972, 1973, 1975, 1977, 1995 by The Lockman Foundation. Used by permission." (www.Lockman.org)

Author has chosen to capitalize certain pronouns that refer to the Godhead, whereas the name of satan and the names associated with him are not capitalized.

Some people's names have been changed to protect the identity of those individuals.

WestBow Press books may be ordered through booksellers or by contacting:

WestBow Press
A Division of Thomas Nelson & Zondervan
1663 Liberty Drive
Bloomington, IN 47403
www.westbowpress.com
1 (866) 928-1240

Because of the dynamic nature of the Internet, any web addresses or links contained in this book may have changed since publication and may no longer be valid. The views expressed in this work are solely those of the author and do not necessarily reflect the views of the publisher, and the publisher hereby disclaims any responsibility for them.

Any people depicted in stock imagery provided by Thinkstock are models, and such images are being used for illustrative purposes only. Certain stock imagery © Thinkstock.

ISBN: 978-1-4908-3129-9 (sc)
ISBN: 978-1-4908-3130-5 (hc)
ISBN: 978-1-4908-3128-2 (e)

Library of Congress Control Number: 2014905431

Printed in the United States of America.

WestBow Press rev. date: 06/27/2014

I dedicate this book to my descendants. I pray for you regularly, including those not yet born. Some of you may never know me, but you can know my story. My hope is that my experiences of Christ will encourage you to take the baton and go to the next levels of faith. As you live expectantly, you will see God do things you never even dreamed possible.

Contents

Acknowledgments

M ike: You are the love of my life and best friend. You have persistently encouraged me to write a book ever since the accident in 1977. When I finally embarked on the journey, you continued to be my greatest cheerleader. You are a gift from heaven.

Our Beloved Children and Grandchildren: Shannon and Rodney, you kicked off this project when you mailed me a new computer and said, "Start writing." You believed it could be done and supported, inspired, and gave suggestions throughout the process. Judah, your precious life was birthed as this project was born. Jason and Chelsea, thank you for giving the thumbs-up and some great editing ideas. I thank God for you, Ella, and Olivia, soon to be born. Candace and Graham, thanks for the prophetic encouragement even years before I began this assignment. I cherish you all—my heartfelt love and thanks beyond words.

Dad: Your life has exemplified the steadfastness of the Lord. You have shown me God's character qualities of trustworthiness and dependability. Thank you for your encouragement in all areas and especially regarding this book. You are a hero to me.

Mom: You are a constant friend and have been a great sounding board. Thank you for your selfless support over the years, for being a great listener, and for reading through all the many rough drafts.

Crystal: What an amazing sister you are. Thanks for standing together to believe for breakthrough after breakthrough.

Colleen and Bob: Thank you for inviting us to the Vineyard in 1981. Your influence has changed our lives forever.

Dear Family: What loyal friends you have been. You and I have walked through these stories together. Jolene, I'm very grateful for your feedback in the final stretch.

Tim: Thank you for all your editing suggestions and the encouraging push to get started.

Brenda: Thank you for opening up the door of the prophetic. You have been an inspiration.

Karen: What an encourager and friend; thanks for the uplifting feedback.

Joanne, Julie, and Tricia: I'm so grateful for your editing expertise and friendship.

Most importantly, I thank you, Father God, Jesus, and Holy Spirit, for your friendship and council. You have walked with me closer than a brother.

Foreword

I have often heard the supposedly humorous comment "Behind every successful man is a great woman."

I know Mike, Cindy's husband, quite well; he is a wonderful man, and now that I have read this book I know why. It is, I am sure, in part (Mike will determine the percentage), attributable to the wonderful woman he married.

I remember Mike telling the story of the train accident to a class that I was teaching when he came in to share his story. I was amazed by the story, but he left out the story of the train driver. I will let you read that for yourself, but it is a clue that this book is full of details that, however well you may think you know Cindy's story, there will be surprises and gems for everyone.

This is a wonderful story of a life lived in faithful obedience. Twice in the book of Romans there is the phrase, "the obedience of faith" (Rom. 1:5 and Rom. 16:26 NASB). I have always loved this phrase, as it brings together the unseen faith and the practical and tangible acts of obedience. It is a marriage of words that sums up this story, for it is one of the obedience of faith. Cindy takes us deep into her life and the lives of her family in such a way that the reader will become a part of the journey and will see the moments of blind faith and the acts of simple trust in a faithful God.

As I read it, I could not avoid referencing in my thoughts my favorite (one of the few that I know) Greek word. It is the Greek word that is translated as endurance in many translations of the Bible. I especially refer to it in the context of Romans 5:4, "and perseverance, proven character and proven character, hope."

The Greek word is *hupomone:* The character of a man unswerved from his deliberate purpose and loyalty to faith and piety by even the greatest trials and sufferings.

How well this definition describes the author.

Finally, I cannot write this foreword without referring to the story of the violin that is threaded through this book. It was for me a sound that echoed through the story, and every time the violin is mentioned, I couldn't wait to see what happened. It spoke to me of passion and hope, and it was as if I could almost hear its sound each time it was mentioned.

I love the verse in Proverbs 13:12, "Hope deferred makes the heart sick, but desire fulfilled is a tree of life." I often think that this verse is misunderstood. It is not that we don't get what we hope for that makes us sick, but it is that we stop hoping. Cindy demonstrates this truth so beautifully. Life and its disappointments could have often given her cause to give up, but as you read, you will hear with me the sound of the violin.

Cindy's story is one of a woman, obedient to faith, who, as a result of that, has developed the *hupomone* character and has never stopped hoping, to such an extent that she has become a minister of hope both in her daily life and in writing this book.

Perseverance, character, hope.

—Paul Manwaring, director of Global Legacy, Bethel Church, Redding, California, and author of *Kisses from a Good God* and *What on Earth Is Glory?* (Destiny Image Publishing)

Preface

In the following pages you'll discover why I and so many others choose to live life with expectancy, no matter what has happened, how long it takes, or what disappointments color the past. My prayer is that you will find renewed hope for all the obstacles that you face today. Things don't have to stay the same. God can surprisingly intervene and turn your difficulty completely around. He is just that good.

> "This is my story, this is my song,
> Praising my Savior all the day long."[i]
> —"Blessed Assurance," Crosby/Knapp

Cindy at Biola University in 1976

Chapter One

The Accident

I woke up to the intensity of ER nurses scurrying around the room. As I lay flat, I heard beeping monitors and people's voices. *Where am I? Could that Amtrak train have hit me? Do I have all my limbs?* Simultaneously, I tried to move my fingers and toes. Although my fingers were attached, two on my left hand were numb. I assumed it was temporary; it had to be. I was a violinist.

Nervously, I strained to recount the blurry details of the accident when I heard my dad's assuring voice at my side. I mumbled, "Dad, I can't believe I wrecked another one of your cars." He comforted me by saying, "Don't worry about the car; that's not important." Then I drifted back into shock.

I was unconscious when the nurse sutured the deep lacerations on both arms, eighty-eight stitches in all. They couldn't give me pain medication, because of the instability of my vital organs.

Earlier that day after finishing my classes at school, I headed to teach private lessons at a local music store as I did every Tuesday afternoon. Feeling the urgency to be on time, I noticed an unusual number of cars lined up as I neared a familiar intersection. A freight train appeared to be parked on the first track of seven. I was in the left-hand turning lane with the cars ahead of me proceeding one at a time. Then it was my turn. Dare I go ahead? The cars behind me were honking, and my heart began to pound. Unsure, I slowly inched toward the intersection. My eye caught a glimpse of the brakeman from the Santa Fe freight train, who began waving to me in a circular motion that I interpreted to mean, "Go ahead." I assumed they were having difficulty with the freight train or the railroad tracks. Slowly I passed the first track and the stopped train, but just as I did, looming above me was the black engine of a second train, the Amtrak. Panicking, I tried to get my car into reverse. That's the last thing I remember.

Witnesses at the scene of the accident later told police that the train crashed into the left front of my car and that the impact shoved me into the crossing guard arm on the right, uprooting the metal pole out of the ground and tossing it to the side. Then my car rammed into the other metal pole, bending it over.

Gas attendants from a nearby station dashed toward the scene to pull me out of the wrecked car. Surprisingly, they discovered the engine had been pushed into the front driver's seat, and I had somehow been thrown into the back with my legs protruding out the rear window. A young woman showed up out of nowhere and said, "Put her on a board in case her back is fractured." Ripping up a shirt from her car, the woman carefully wrapped a tourniquet around the area above my left elbow. Blood was pouring out like a faucet. Since the ambulance took over twenty minutes to arrive, witnesses said she likely kept me from bleeding to death.

That Tuesday, instead of leaving home right before work, this young woman named Debbie left an hour early, placing her car behind mine at the scene of the accident. Surprisingly, she was an acquaintance of mine from college but didn't recognize me because of all the swelling and bleeding. Although naturally squeamish, Debbie had recently taken first-aid training at our school, Biola University, and she took charge at the scene with all the confidence of a professional.

Once in the ambulance, my friend shared the gospel with me. She knew that I was unconscious but hoped that somehow I heard her words. The next day in chapel, she was shocked to discover that she had helped a friend.

I lay motionless and pale on the ER gurney while the doctor told my parents, "The X-rays show a spinal fracture, multiple fractures to the skull, and a shattered shoulder. She severed the ulnar nerve right above the left elbow, causing the numbness and loss of dexterity to her hand. Since she lost so much blood, we're giving her a blood transfusion and are monitoring her internal injuries. However, I can't assure you that she'll make it through the night. We're doing all we can."

College students flooded the waiting room to pray. My parents received a visitor in the hospital, who was carrying a Bible, and introduced himself as the Amtrak train engineer involved in the accident. "I noticed the pages of your daughter's Bible strewn around her car at the scene, and I've come to bring her a new Bible with healing verses underlined," he said. Then he added, "I felt impressed by the Lord to tell you, 'Don't worry, your daughter will be healed.'" He handed my parents a gold-colored Good News Bible. When they opened it, the cover read

"To Cindy," followed by his signature. The next page had four healing verses scribbled at the top, each one shakily underlined in the text.

The Amtrak engineer left as quickly as he came, and my parents were back in ICU staring into reality as I lay silent under the influence of strong pain medication. The nurses had tubes going through my nose and down my throat and IVs in my arms. My fiancé Mike brushed the curtain aside and peeked into my dark Intensive Care Unit before entering. Immediately, the nurse chased him out of the room when she noticed my heart monitor go wild. "Who are you?" she asked. "You're causing too much excitement. You'll have to wait until she's more stable."

When the pain medication wore off, I felt tormented. I was alone in the darkness; the sounds of the monitors continued to beep. My mind was racing. My legs periodically shot in the air because of muscle spasms, and the tube going down my throat made swallowing painful. I wondered how long I could tolerate it all. Finally, the Demerol shot took affect again, and I dozed off to sleep.

Five days later, new X-rays were taken. There was no trace of the fractures in my lower back and skull! The doctors were shocked and initially tried to explain it away. But X-rays don't lie, and they finally admitted to my dad, "We don't understand what happened." Dad replied, "This is a miracle. Thousands of people were praying for her, and God did the impossible."

Since my vitals had stabilized and my fractures were now gone, I no longer needed the extensive care offered in ICU. So that same day, a staff person wheeled my bed down a long hall and up an elevator into a large, well-lit room. When he dropped my bruised body onto the fresh white sheets of my new bed, I cried out for another pain shot.

Because of the internal injuries, the cardiac ward was my new home. With the fractures healed, the doctors focused on the internal damage. I don't remember when they told my parents, "There's a good chance that your daughter will never be able to have children because of the injuries." Two months before the collision, I had agreed to marry Mike Wenger, a guy I met in freshman English. We talked about the dreams of our future family, but now were faced with this daunting possibility of infertility.

Once settled in my new room, the nurse handed me my glasses and pointed to a large yellow poster on the wall. "Look at all the get-well wishes from your friends. The doctors and nurses are calling you Bionic Woman and Wonder Woman," she said as she began reading some of the messages on the poster. Her voice trailed off as I drifted back to sleep.

I woke up to the sound of my mother's gentle voice beside my bed. "Are you hungry?" She pointed to my lunch on the tray. Here I was at age twenty, not able to use either arm, so Mom began to spoon-feed me. I asked, "Where's Dad?" Mom hesitated before answering. What was she to say? Dad had just informed her that he felt too sick to come to the hospital. That morning, he had surveyed the damage to my mutilated car and noticed a hunk of my hair in the back seat, enough to make an entire braid. He stayed home traumatized and nauseous. She simply said, "He won't be coming today. He's not feeling very well." Exhausted herself, she continued to serve me and lingered at my bedside.

Later that afternoon, all alone in my room, I began reflecting on all that had happened. By then, I knew that my left ulnar nerve had been severed above my elbow. The numbness in my two left hand fingers and hand was not a temporary condition. Since the age of nine, my life's passion was to be a concert violinist, and I was well on my way at twenty years of age. I had anticipated that the following year I'd be the concertmistress of our university orchestra. My love for the instrument and my desire to be a violinist had become my identity.

The sun shone through the window above me as I lay in my hospital bed. I stared at the fresh black stitches on my right arm and felt thankful none were on my face. One group of stitches on my forearm resembled a rainbow, reminding me of the promises of God. I couldn't believe I survived a train accident and felt anticipation as I contemplated my future destiny. Surely, since God had healed my back and skull, he would also heal my severed nerve.

The next day, the atmosphere felt strange and almost electric as I tried to move my right arm. I felt an unusual thrill in the pit of my stomach. "Look, I can move it halfway up!" I told my parents. I knew I felt something different in the atmosphere, a good feeling, but I didn't know then that it was the Holy Spirit.

The following day, I stretched my right arm completely up, and the next day I sat up in my bed. The doctors and nurses continued to be amazed as each day brought improvement. By day nine, I slowly got up from my bed and walked to the bathroom. Visitors regularly brought gifts and bouquets of flowers that decorated the room and gave it the aroma of a floral shop.

Eleven days after the accident, the doctors released me from the hospital. I felt loved and cherished by God and anxious to go home. I walked out the double doors with a sling supporting my left shoulder and arm. Much of my body was healed, but the ligaments and tendons in my arm were a tangled mess and a sling supported my recovering shattered shoulder. Since I had severed my ulnar nerve right above the elbow, I was scheduled for surgery in two months. But somehow, this day, May 7, 1977, I wasn't concerned about all that; I enjoyed the fresh sunny spring air as my parents walked me to the car.

My sister and friend with the car—before and after the accident

Chapter Two

Rays of Hope

P eeking into the window of the last practice room off the long hallway, I stood and stared for what seemed like several minutes. I watched one of my fellow violinists from our university orchestra practice her music. My heart sank. It had only been three weeks since the accident, but I didn't expect all the overwhelming emotion as I visited my familiar music hall. Pangs of grief set in as I thought about my future. *Who am I now, and what am I going to do with my life?*

Upon coming home, I painstakingly tried to play my violin but could only play pieces I played in junior high. I closed the case and stored away my instrument. My life seemed like scattered pieces of a jigsaw puzzle. At times, my emotions vacillated from thankfulness to grief. I felt thankful to be alive and excited about my December wedding, but simultaneously I felt the deep loss of my dreams. For the last eleven years I had invested my heart, time, and energy into the ambition of being a concert violinist.

Two weeks later my friend Debbie, who saved my life at the accident, invited me to sing at her wedding. I felt encouraged to have something to practice, something to do. The fact that God gave me the energy and ability to perform so soon after the accident gave me a level of fulfillment and brought praise and glory to the Healer Himself.

It was May, and I needed to make a decision about the following fall semester at school. Although it was a long shot,

I decided to try to finish up my music degree with a voice emphasis instead of violin. This meant lots of catch-up with hours of practicing to get ready for a senior recital in just a year and a half. But it was motivating to have a new challenge, and I began suppressing my feelings of disappointment.

Time for Surgery

Two months later I sat in my stale white hospital room, feeling lonely and nervous but anticipating a healing in my fingers. Weeks ago, a neurosurgeon explained that he was going to tie my median nerve to what was left of the ulnar nerve to prevent atrophy of the muscles in my left arm. The surgery would also give me a fifty percent chance of regaining feeling in my fingers. Experiencing all the miracles God had already performed, I anticipated the good outcome.

As I waited for nurses to come and prep me for surgery, I noticed that the hospital smells and sounds were all too familiar. I took out a book to read but couldn't concentrate.

Finally, after four hours on the operating table, it was all over. The anesthesia wore off, and I opened my eyes. The room was dimly lit, and I noticed it was dark outside. I looked over to see my parents' tired but encouraging faces. The smell of the hospital food made me nauseous, but the nurse urged me to eat. "Your surgery took four hours," said my dad with his usual uplifting voice. "The surgeon had to untangle so many tendons and ligaments that it was quite the ordeal.

But now you should be able to move your arm around and use it just fine. The doctor said it could be months before we know if the nerve will regenerate all the way down to your fingers. He said to give it at least six months. Nerves heal slowly." Wow, more waiting. I was hoping that I could see immediate results.

A few months after surgery, I stood behind a table in the back of a large church selling our family's musical albums. I had performed music together with my family since I was four, and we still ministered in churches about once a week. I explained to the people with excitement in my voice, "My nerve has regenerated almost down to my wrist, and my hopes are that I will soon be able to feel the strings on my violin."

But when the nerve function didn't return to my hand, I turned all my attention toward practicing voice for hours, studying for my classes, and preparing for my December wedding. I changed my mind on wedding colors three times. I didn't know how to deal with the disappointment. After all, shouldn't I just be happy that God spared my life from a tragic accident?

Not only had I stored my violin away, but I also wouldn't even listen to string music. I must have thought I could just start a completely new chapter in my life. Out with the old and in with the new. I didn't realize until years later that my new coping mechanism was simply to stuff down my grief and disappointment and try to be strong. In the early days, I knew little about living a life of expectancy. I figured if God hadn't healed me by now, I wouldn't be healed. The elders of our Dutch Reformed Church had laid hands on me and nothing happened, so I would simply move on.

Eight months after the accident, just as planned, Mike and I celebrated our dream wedding with a bell choir, pipe organ, violin, guitar, and singers. Looking through the glass wall of our Dutch Reformed Church, I could see the colored fountains springing up from the ground as the sun began to set.

Married life was wonderful. The two of us continued our education and pastored the junior high kids at church. We were happy, eating together by candlelight almost every night in our little apartment. It didn't matter if we ate hot dogs or steak— though it was mostly hot dogs.

Graduation

I looked forward to my voice lessons every week. God handpicked the perfect teacher for me, a robust man with a deep, resounding voice that had just the right combination of compassion and motivational skills. I sang in a couple of short recitals before I eventually learned thirty minutes of music in three languages for my senior recital. A couple of months later, Mike and I graduated from the university. Walking the aisle together, we received our diplomas.

What about Children?

The fact that Mike didn't break our engagement when he heard from the doctor that I probably wouldn't be able to have children is a credit to his commitment to me. He just assumed, as did I, that when the time came, we would adopt children.

After a couple of years of marriage, the desire for children grew. Remembering the doctor's words at the time of the accident, we talked and dreamed about adopting. Everywhere I looked, my eyes seemed to focus on the babies and little children.

One morning, two years after our wedding, feeling some unusual symptoms, I bought a pregnancy test. The test showed positive; I felt elated and couldn't wait to give the news to Mike. But my excitement was short-lived as I lost the baby that same day.

When I confided with an older woman at our church about the miscarriage, she said, "Honey, you can have more children; you're very young and it's probably for the best." I expected more compassion; her words felt callous.

That spring the Lord opened up a teaching opportunity for me in a large private school. My attention was diverted for a time to lesson plans and performances. I taught music appreciation to elementary and middle school kids and directed band and choir. Mike took a position as youth pastor in Fountain Valley and taught social studies at Whittier High School. We arrived home every night exhausted and would prop up our feet on the coffee table and eat frozen dinners.

One year later, as I exited a fertility specialist's office, the receptionist stamped the word *infertile* on my form and handed it to me. Within days of that visit, we conceived our first baby. From the beginning, the doctor labeled the pregnancy high-risk, and he kept close watch during the next few months.

Suddenly, five weeks early, I began premature labor and was admitted into the hospital where the doctor gave me medication through an IV to stop the contractions. It worked. Three weeks later, our precious son, Jason Michael, arrived, weighing a healthy eight pounds and two ounces.

The nurse handed him to me and said, "What a beautiful California beach baby. He looks like he could be a football player someday." I couldn't take my eyes off of his perfect face, big blue eyes and blond hair. Instantly I loved my new role as mother.

God's Word Overrides Man's

My four-year journey of learning to live in expectancy had begun. I was beginning to see that when circumstances appear bleak, all hope is not lost. Doctors had initially warned my parents that I might not survive the accident. A day later they said I might never walk and could be in the hospital for six months. Finally, they said I had probably lost the ability to have children. Although they were wrong on all three counts, it's no discredit to the medical field. God simply performed supernaturally. His Word overrides man's word.

In the natural, I was told that I was barren, but God replaced the infertility with fruitfulness. I realized that the same could be true in the spiritual realm. Our God can transform any area of barrenness. Even when others say our circumstances are hopeless or when we feel imprisoned or abandoned, He is able to bring fruitfulness to any situation physically and spiritually.

Learning to see past my circumstances was the first step in my journey to live life expecting God's goodness.

Chapter Three

Learning in the Journey

Healing for Our Baptist Boys

O ne night, not long after we both turned twenty-five, Mike bounded into the kitchen and said, "Two of the guys in the youth group just got back from a Teen Missions retreat, and they say they got healed. They threw away all the medications they were taking—don't need them anymore." Then he added, "But now they're speaking in tongues and saying that they had an experience with the Holy Spirit." I looked at him in surprise. This was our second year as youth pastors of a small Baptist church near the beach in Southern California. Even though we were glad the boys were healed, neither of us wanted to see our young people turning charismatic on us. Then Mike said, "Now their parents are begging me to try to talk their sons out of this whole experience." We had no idea how much upheaval this one incident was going to cause.

Worship Was a Key

Ironically, within weeks of this healing episode, Mike and I were invited to visit a church that met in a Yorba Linda gymnasium. It was called Calvary Chapel of Yorba Linda and later renamed Vineyard Christian Fellowship. Our brother-in-law Bob said, "When these people worship, you can tell that they really mean it! You guys have to come and visit with us.

The pastor's name is John Wimber." The more Bob talked, the more we felt a hunger deep down inside. At our young age, Mike and I were already feeling tired in ministry. We argued all the way to church, put on our happy faces when we entered the foyer, and tried to persuade our youth to get excited about Jesus. They didn't want to sing; they sat in their chairs staring at us with blank looks on their faces, seemingly saying, "When will all this be over?" Underneath the façade, I thought the same thing.

It was a Sunday night. I handed our precious baby to a lady in the nursery of the Vineyard Church, and we entered the large gymnasium. Not only were the bleachers filled but also nearly all the seats in the middle. We spotted four chairs in a row near the back and slid over to claim them. Bob, Colleen (Bob's wife), Mike, and I scanned the room sprinkled with all different kinds of people from a variety of cultures, ethnic groups, and social standing. Suddenly the sound of guitars strumming interrupted our silent observations. Bob pointed to an older gray-haired gentleman wearing safari shorts standing behind the keyboard. "That's John Wimber, the pastor," he said as the worship leader started to sing.

During worship, my eyes drifted from person to person. Many of their faces seemed to glow as they worshiped God with such intimacy and passion. It seemed as if they were having an experience that was deeper than anything I had known. Something was different here, and I wanted to find out what it was. I didn't realize I had already embarked on the next phase of my new journey—to discover more about ministering to Jesus in my worship.

I had heard it said, "Experience isn't important." But I knew that experience played a vital role in my marriage relationship, and I desired more of an encounter with the Lord than I had in the past. It was time to really get to know His love for me. I began to worship on a deeper level. Instead of halfhearted worship, I stepped out to give more of myself in surrender to the Lord. Even as I lifted my hands in worship, I noticed more freedom. I allowed the words of the songs and the presence of God to go deeper in my spirit, and I had a new awareness of His pleasure over me. Over time, I started to feel a greater connection with Father God and I could hear His voice speaking to me. I read John 4:23, which said, "the true worshipers will worship the Father in spirit and truth." I noticed that when I joined my heart with His in worship, my discouragement would leave, and I felt uplifted. I couldn't get enough. I was giving Him my praise and worship, but I was definitely receiving back more than what I was giving.

Pray Once; Pray Twice

John Wimber's brother-in-law, Bob Fulton, met with us often, answering questions about the gifts of the Spirit. We searched the Scripture, studied church history, and read about men like George Fox from the 1600s. We felt like kids in a candy store as a whole new world of adventure opened up to us. The more we read, the more we realized that since the resurrection of Christ, many have seen the demonstration of God's power. We studied how revival in the Great Awakenings changed people's hearts and changed the culture of the day. Bob quoted verses like Hebrews 13:8, "Jesus Christ is the same yesterday, today, and forever." Some of the parts of the Bible that we thought were just history came alive to us as we discovered we could live like that now.

Pastor Bob invited us to a small group that he was leading, and we visited one Tuesday night. The house was charged with about sixty young people in their twenties that crowded the hallways and various rooms. Mike and I, along with Bob and Colleen, hid behind a large indoor palm tree to make us a bit more inconspicuous. We had no idea what to expect.

Finally, everyone gathered in the spacious living room. I noticed that over the large brick fireplace hung a mirror that covered the entire wall. Straight ahead was a winding oak staircase filled with young people. A young woman sat cross-legged with her guitar in the middle of the floor and led us into about forty-five minutes of worship. I could feel the stress leave my body as the presence of God swept through the room. It drew my attention away from my nervousness toward the love and kindness of the Lord.

This was followed by a minute of silence. Then a young man said, "There are two women here. Your names both start with the letter *C*." And although he had never met us, he proceeded to share things about Colleen and I that he could never have known. I thought, *I guess there's no hiding here.* I felt singled out and valued by God.

A couple of months later, the leader directed some of us into the kitchen to pray for an older gentleman with cancer of the tongue. He was scheduled to have surgery to remove part of his tongue in just a few weeks. What made it even worse was this man was a professional saxophone player. We all laid hands on him and prayed, but since this healing prayer was new to Mike and me, we mostly watched.

The next week, the sick man reported that he had a little more feeling in his tongue, so we prayed again. Week after week, there was just a little more improvement. His taste buds returned gradually, one food at a time. Eventually, after months of soaking prayer, the doctor gave him a clean bill of health. We gained more confidence in God's ability to heal, whether quickly or gradually.

I had always thought that if a person wasn't healed immediately, it probably wasn't the right timing, or maybe it wasn't going to happen at all. But this Vineyard pastor showed us in Scripture that even Jesus, in the gospels, prayed twice for the blind man in Bethsaida before he was completely healed, setting an example for believers to persist in prayer (Mark 8:24).

Back to the Baptist Youth Group

One night, back with our church's youth group, Mike and I were chatting at a social hosted by the parents of one of our teens. I was dishing food onto my plate when my eyes glanced over to a guitar leaning up against the wall. I hadn't tried to play since my instrument was shredded in the train accident four years earlier. I set down my food and reached over to grab the well-worn guitar. After stepping into a quiet bedroom, I shut the door, and to my amazement, I could play several chords. My fingers were probably growing a little stronger with the exercises I had done on the piano. A light flashed on in my head. *I might not be able to play violin, but I'm going to buy a new guitar and lead worship.* A few weeks later, I did just that.

We continued to visit the Vineyard small group, and our new experiences influenced how we led our Baptist youth group. We started to add songs that were directed *to* God and not just *about* Him. And instead of pressuring the kids to sing loud and get excited, we simply began to worship God ourselves. When we did, the presence of the Lord would fill the place. The kids responded with a fresh desire to seek after God. The striving was gone, and the youth grew in intimacy with the Lord.

When the young people arrived at youth group with injuries, sickness, or emotional pain, they asked for prayer. We would gather around to lay hands on them for healing. Some were healed, and the ones that weren't still felt the love of the Lord. Everything seemed to be going so well.

The Importance of Forgiveness

One day, our Baptist pastor called Mike into his office. Instead of starting with small talk, he simply said, "Mike, I've noticed that you and Cindy are singing a long time with the young people on Sunday morning—too long." My husband braced himself for what followed. "We want you to just sing a couple of songs instead of going on for half an hour. The second thing is we'd like you to stop laying hands on the sick." Then he gave the ultimatum. "If you don't go back to how things used to be, you'll have to leave the church." Mike was quiet for a moment and then asked, "So you don't want us to have any healing time with the young people?" The pastor responded, "We believe that God heals who He wants to heal, but we don't want the practice of healing or laying on of hands." Shaken, Mike responded softly, "Okay, I'll talk to Cindy and give you a phone call."

Looking back, we might have been a bit naïve, but we were astonished that we were being asked to leave if we wanted to continue down the path that brought so much life and growth in our own lives. Surely there was some misunderstanding. The following day, when Mike talked with the pastor and shared our conviction to pray for healing, the pastor carefully laid out the instructions for us to follow the upcoming Sunday. And we were thrust into a season that tested our faith.

Sunday came. We taught the Sunday school class with butterflies in our stomachs and an ache in our hearts. As we said our good-byes to the kids, we knew this was our last day. But as the pastor instructed, we didn't tell them we were leaving. They would find out we were gone in the following service. I tried to hold back the tears. *Surely God, this is just a bad dream. Maybe You will still turn things around.*

Right after Sunday school we walked into the foyer and noticed the pastor's daughter. We rushed over to hug her. Besides the associate pastor, she was the only other person that knew we were leaving; and she and her boyfriend were our best friends. We all shed tears as we embraced and said our good-byes. I thought, *Surely we will continue our relationship. This difference in our beliefs should not cut off our friendship.* But even though we tried to continue to connect, this was the last day we ever saw her, the pastor, or anyone from that church. I remember walking out the double doors of the fellowship hall that last time, carrying our five-month-old son. Mike was walking directly behind me. We had no clue what was ahead or how the bills would be paid. Although our faith was small, we trusted God would provide. We felt the pain of this loss but knew He was with us. The process of forgiveness began that day. It was a choice of our will, not a feeling. And since we had so recently believed exactly like they did, it was easier to forgive these friends.

We knew that forgiveness would be another key in learning to stay expectant in our own journey. Bitterness would dampen hope and keep us from God's purposes. Oddly enough as we exited the Baptist church, I remember feeling a bit of excitement as I thought, *Wow, God, what's next?*

Surprised with Holy Spirit

The following week, Mike dug ditches part time at the Vineyard Christian Fellowship office property. One warm spring day while he shoveled dirt for a telephone wire, he heard a voice say, "Hi, I'm Lonnie Frisbee. I heard that you're the Baptist boy." Trembling, Mike looked up, leaning against his shovel. This was the prophet he had heard so much about. *What if Lonnie prays for me and I fall down in this ditch? No one would ever find me,* he thought. "Yes, I am," Mike answered timidly. With a twinkle in his eye, Lonnie continued, "Well, this Sunday you and your wife are going to get baptized in the Spirit. So get ready." Before Mike could respond, Lonnie was gone.

The service ended that Sunday night, and people filed to the side room for prayer. I felt a bit nervous as we joined the others. Walking through the doorway I noticed Lonnie had people gathered around him. Mike and I were separated into different groups, and a few ladies approached me. Before long, just has had been prophesied, I experienced the presence of God flow throughout my entire being as I was baptized in the Holy Spirit. The Lord had prepared our minds and hearts for this new experience. We had asked lots of questions and studied Scripture on the gifts of the Holy Spirit. We read in Acts 8 that the believers in Jerusalem had already experienced being baptized into the *name* of the Lord Jesus. But when the apostles laid hands on them, they received the Holy Spirit in a fresh way. In Acts 10, the gift of the Holy Spirit was poured out while Peter was preaching. But this time, no one even laid hands on them. We had read these Scriptures and others many times before and were ready for this new experience with God.

Mike received his prayer language the moment his group prayed for him, but I was too afraid to let any weird sounds come out of my mouth. So instead of pressuring or manipulating me, the lady said, "Just step out in the quiet of your own home and speak out whatever syllables come to you."

When I arrived home, I walked outside in the warm summer night air and paced up and down the sidewalk. I just let syllables flow out of my mouth. Since it sounded like baby talk, I struggled with doubt, thinking my tongue language wasn't real—that is until God showed up in a powerful way about a year later. But I knew this baptism was monumental. There was a new passion that burned on the inside of me, and it lit a fire that began to blaze from that moment on.

Not long after, Mike landed a full-time job with a financial planner. But right after we had spent most of our first check on groceries, the phone rang. I answered it. "Ma'am, is this Cynthia Wenger?" "Yes, it is," I answered with caution. The man proceeded to tell me, "The check you recently spent at our grocery store has bounced." Confused, I said, "I will look into it. I can't understand why there would be a problem." I quickly called Mike. *What was this about?*

Mike's boss at the financial planning company was a believer and attended our new church, but we were soon informed that the business had gone under. The man felt terrible and promised to repay us, but it never happened. Now we faced another choice to forgive. It was a struggle at first. After all, we had forgiven our Baptist church, left quietly, and trusted God for finances. Shouldn't we be blessed for that right away?

I guess I thought I deserved my reward right then and there, not another disappointment.

Blessings Ahead

Before we could even mourn the loss of the last job, Mike landed work at Lucky's Bakery in Orange County. And although we never got paid from the financial planner, the blessings started pouring in.

After several months, a surprise phone call changed everything. I was spooning the last bite of baby food into our son's mouth when I noticed Mike standing in the kitchen doorway. He grinned from ear to ear. "Pastor Bob just asked me to come on staff at the Vineyard working with youth and small groups," he said. What a surprise. Mike hadn't applied for this position, nor did he know it existed.

This was a dream come true, to partner with a movement of God that was radically changing us and those around us. One hundred or more youth were getting saved every week. Home groups formed continually. The place was rich with opportunity, life, growth, and advancement. Healing was the norm, and we would arrive at church about an hour early just to get a good seat to hear our pastor, John Wimber. It was common to experience the presence of the Lord throughout the service.

One Sunday evening, our pastor said, "Someone just stole a wallet, and you need to return it and come up front and repent." Suddenly a young teenager bounded down the bleachers and ran to the front, throwing the wallet to the ground. This was definitely not church as usual.

The Lord would speak to me in such tender ways as I worshiped Him at church as well as at home. Faith was stirred in my heart to expect God to do extraordinary things. Every Sunday John would share about the miracles, healings, and encounters with people that he had during the week. It was so contagious that we all expected to experience God's supernatural power. I didn't understand that this was a movement of God, and it would impact the church at large. I assumed that all charismatic churches were like this.

Mike and I felt grateful to be back in ministry again, learning and growing.

Your Children Will Be Seated Around Your Table

One day Pastor Bob's wife brought a team of women to pray for me in my home. She prophesied to me by saying, "Your children [will be] like olive plants All around your table" (Ps. 128:3b). I immediately thought, *One son couldn't be seated around a table. God must be giving us more children.* It was only months until I was pregnant with our second child, and we were thrilled. Being a high-risk pregnancy, the last two months challenged me as the doctor prescribed total bed rest. This was no easy task since our active son was now two years of age. But thankfully we all survived those few months.

For some reason, I was convinced that we were having another son, enough so that we bought bunk beds for the boys. So when the doctor said, "It's a girl," Mike and I were completely but pleasantly surprised. We named her Shannon Joy after our pastor's daughter and my sister. She had lots of brown hair with a tint of auburn, deep blue eyes, and a delicate, thin frame. She put her thumb in her mouth the instant she was laid on my chest. Overjoyed, I cuddled our second miracle child.

Body Life

During this new season, often people would pray in faith for a creative miracle for my left hand. I felt anticipation. Although I didn't experience healing, they imparted new faith.

We practiced body-life like never before as we started home groups and developed strong relationships. It became clear that a healthy Christian needs a community of close-knit friends. This was another key in our journey to live life expecting the power of God. To stay encouraged and strengthened in the faith was so much easier when we weren't alone.

The kingdom of God was coming to earth. We often prayed, "Your kingdom come. Your will be done ..." (Matt. 6:10). Our faith in God's ability grew as we laid hands on people and they were healed emotionally and physically. When we felt discouraged or disappointed, there was always someone to lift us up. It was in this community, under apostolic leadership, that our hearts grew softer, our love grew stronger, and our faith was stirred. Ephesians 4:16 took on new meaning. We were becoming "joined and knit together." Christ, our head, was healing areas of brokenness in all of us, and we were learning the joy of being God's friend, living in His presence, and trusting His people. In this positive environment, when God didn't answer our prayers in our timing, we could more easily stay strong and persevere through life's difficulties. It became easier to believe that our best days were ahead. We had never had such a large support group, and it became clear to us that if the devil can separate people from the rest of the body, he can more easily persuade them to give up. In the Ephesians passage I referred to earlier, Paul says, "but, speaking the truth in love, may grow up in all things into Him who is the head— Christ—from whom the whole body, joined and knit together by what every joint supplies, according to the effective working by which every part does its share, causes growth of the body for the edifying of itself in love" (Eph. 4:15-16).

Surprised with the Gift of Tongues

About a year later our friend's home was crowded with twenty-year-olds seeking after God. A few people sat on the furniture and the rest of us were cross-legged on the floor while a friend and I led worship. Everyone was so hungry for God that the presence of the Lord filled the small living room. One young man asked for prayer. Mike and I and a few others walked over to lay hands on him and pray. I prayed quietly in my tongue language before stepping out in English. After a while, I felt a soft touch on my shoulder and looked over to see a young woman, about twenty, motioning me to come to the side.

"Do you know what you were saying when you prayed in tongues?" asked this visitor. "No, I have no idea," I responded. Then she proceeded to tell me. "Since my parents were missionaries in Italy, I know quite a few Italian dialects. You were saying, 'My God, dear one of my heart,' in Italian. You said it over and over, and I can even tell you the exact dialect you were speaking." Amazed, I replied, "Wow, I can't believe it!" Then she asked, "Would you and your husband lay hands on me so I can receive the gift of tongues?" Right then, God poured out His love on this young woman and filled her with the Baptism of the Holy Spirit and the gift of tongues.

I began to use my prayer language more than ever and noticed that even though my mind usually didn't know what I was saying, my inner man was strengthened every time.

A Miracle on the Way

On Shannon's first birthday, much to our surprise, my pregnancy test showed positive once again. It was 1985, and we had since moved up to Albany, Oregon. I had always wanted three children, and everything progressed normally until three weeks before the due date.

I woke up suddenly. Something was wrong. The room was dark; it was about three o'clock in the morning. When Mike turned on the overhead light, we saw blood all over the bed. I couldn't feel the baby move and began to panic. Mike called 911, and some friends drove over to watch the other children. With towels wrapped all around me, I nervously lay in the ambulance as we sped off toward the hospital.

Once we arrived, the sonogram showed that the placenta had detached, causing all the bleeding. The baby was fine. After giving me some medication, I was sent home to wait for labor to begin. A few hours later, the contractions intensified, and we rushed back to the Corvallis hospital.

Even with the complications, I delivered Candace Noel at seven pounds and two ounces. She was healthy with very light blonde, almost white hair and blue eyes. In spite of the predictions of infertility, we now had three beautiful children that survived high-risk pregnancies, and we felt blessed. The Scripture came to pass. "Your children like olive plants All around your table" (Ps. 128:3b).

Feeling the Grief

After Candace was born, Mike left full-time ministry and was hired at United Parcel Service. Our lives took a 180 degree turn. At first, we were just excited to be making more money. But once Mike was promoted to management, the work became more strenuous and the hours were long. It wasn't that my husband didn't spend time with the kids and me; the little time he had off was spent at home. But life seemed more meaningless and mundane. The phone wasn't ringing; people didn't need us. We had never experienced a season like this. Some days we wondered if UPS was a mistake. Had we gotten off course? But every time Mike searched for a different job, the door closed.

One afternoon, when our children were away in elementary school, Mike and I chatted at the breakfast table. He asked me, "What do you think about our family ministering in some churches in the area? You could share your testimony and our family could sing?" About twelve years had elapsed now since the accident, and we were in our mid-thirties, feeling like life was ebbing away. So shortly after Mike's brainstorm, our family headed to Corvallis, Oregon, for the first program. Our three kids were dressed up in their Sunday best, and the van was packed with my music equipment and guitar.

We arrived at a Baptist church, where an old friend from Biola University was pastoring at the time. After our ministry, we expected the pastor to simply end the service. But as our family walked down to sit in the front row, he proceeded to tell the congregation how he had been privileged to hear me play violin back in the college days. He continued, "The atmosphere was full of the presence of God when she played." His words caught me completely off guard, and I didn't expect what followed.

Suddenly, the dam broke. Although I had experienced some level of emotional healing, the Lord was now unraveling a new layer. I couldn't keep the tears from running down my cheeks. I felt embarrassed since it had been so many years since the accident, and now here I was falling apart in front of these people. Feelings of grief and anger surfaced as I thought about how my gift had seemingly been ripped away at such a young age. *God, why would You allow this talent to be stolen from me, especially when it brought You glory?* I quickly pulled myself together, and strangely enough, I felt the love of the Lord wash over me.

Grief was a part of the process. And often, as was happening in my case, sorrow is released in layers. I had to allow myself to feel the loss so that I could move ahead into the joy, the freedom, and the expectation for the future.

Shortly after this experience, God enrolled me in a new class. It was time to learn another valuable lesson that would prove to help keep hope alive time and time again in my future. My journey had only just begun.

Chapter Four

Thankfulness

After a long day, Mike walked in the door around eight o'clock in the evening. Exhausted from work, he headed to bed early. I tucked the kids into bed and felt a tug at my heart to spend some time alone with God, so I knelt down beside the couch in our small living room. The house was silent, and the room was dark. Praying aloud, I poured out my heart to the Lord. "God, are You pleased with me? I want to please You and be more connected to *You*. How do *You* want to use me?" I felt a hunger in my heart for more of God and desperately wanted to hear His voice. Immediately, I heard in my spirit, *Read 1 Corinthians, chapter ten.* Turning on a lamp, I began to scan the verses. I had no idea what I was going to find.

In this passage, Paul refers to the Old Testament example of the children of Israel wandering through the wilderness. My eyes fell on verse ten, "nor complain, as some of them also complained...." Some translations say they "grumbled." To complain is the opposite of being thankful. The children of Israel weren't pleasing God because of their lack of thankfulness.

When I set my Bible down, the Holy Spirit filled the room with His presence, and I was overcome with His love. He began touching my heart in a deep way as I repented for the many times I had focused on the negative circumstances instead of being grateful. I knew that this night was a new beginning. I felt sorrow at first; then it transformed into joy.

That Sunday, our pastor's wife started a series of teachings on the importance of being thankful. Week after week, I sat on the edge of my seat, taking notes. She explained, using Scripture and stories, how to transition from negativity to possessing a thankful heart. For the first time in my life, I understood that there were thoughts that assaulted my mind that simply weren't mine to keep. God could help me become a manager of those thoughts, deciding which could stay and which had to go (2 Cor. 10:5). The Lord began to reveal to me that my spirit-man needed to grow stronger and become more mature. Feeding my spirit the Word of God was the healthiest food available. I spent time meditating on Scripture and cultivating truth in my inner person. Gradually, I was able to make the choice to be thankful.

I became aware that throughout Scripture God gives us many tools that can help a person bear up amidst oppression and negativity. God had taught me the value of worship, forgiveness, and many other things, but now he added this—let your mind entertain thankful thoughts.

This attitude adjustment was like putting on a new pair of glasses or like trimming an unruly lawn. My prayers changed. Instead of begging, pleading prayers all the time, I began to thank the Lord for the breakthrough before it happened. I was learning to see the answer from the position of the finished work on the cross. When circumstances looked hopeless, I shouted out declarations: "Thank You, Jesus, that You are going to bring the deliverance I need." When my thoughts changed, my words changed. Jesus said, "A good man out of the good treasure of his heart brings forth good; and an evil man out of the evil treasure of his heart brings forth evil. For out of the abundance of the heart his mouth speaks" (Luke 6:45).

It was time to incorporate an attitude of thanksgiving and praise into my daily living. It was usually a sacrifice at first as I battled discouragement, pain, or other opposition. But just like David, the pleading prayers were not nonexistent; they were just coupled with hope and praise. Then surprisingly, I would notice that often I felt uplifted even before I saw the breakthrough come in the natural.

Soon I was faced with a trial that put the lesson to the test. If you've experienced anxiety in your life as I have, you may be able to relate to the next story.

Surprise Visitor

It had been a couple of years since the Lord spoke to me about thankfulness when I had a surprise visitor. I heard a strong knock and felt a chill as I opened the door to an unfamiliar face. "I'm here to serve you papers," said a woman without emotion. She handed me a folder and continued, "I can't answer any of your questions, but you can talk to your lawyer." Suddenly, my heart seemed to be in my throat. *There must be some mistake,* I thought as I opened the folder to carefully examine the contents. My visitor was gone as quickly as she came. All alone, I said, "What is this? I'm being sued? For what?" The air felt suffocating as I read further and saw the amount was $85,000 plus an indefinite amount of money to cover this lady's medical problems.

Two years earlier I had rear-ended a woman as I was driving my kids to piano lessons. It was a minor fender bender, and I presumed my insurance company had settled it months ago. Our collision insurance policy was only $50,000 at the time, and this lady hadn't settled for that amount in the last two year time period. In addition, she claimed to have many severe injuries from this accident.

My mind wandered back to the scene, and I remembered the woman and I talked and exchanged information on the side of the road. It had been so long ago, the details were foggy, but the damage to both of our vehicles' fenders was so minor that I hadn't given it further thought.

On the other end of the line, the insurance office receptionist said, "Yes, she had many preexisting problems, but this could still be a difficult case for you since you were at fault." My heart sank and anxiety gripped me again. After hanging up the phone, I attempted to give God my fear, but I just couldn't find peace. I asked Him, *God, how does this work? Do You defend Your people when it's their fault?* I felt upset with myself. But what I heard back was, "Give Me thanks; just praise Me."

I was in the heat of the battle over the following weeks and months. Since we didn't have much of a savings, I worried we might lose the house. Each time the lawyer pressed me to recall the details of the accident, my anxiety grew. He pitched questions to me right and left. "How fast were you going? Where exactly was the collision?" The lawyer and I actually drove to the scene of the accident, and he asked, "When and where did you start to put on the brakes?" *What do you mean, when did I put on the brakes?* I thought, *It's been two years!* The details were hazy. So I prayed, *Lord, help me.* Again, the only thing I heard from God was, "Thank Me for what I'm about to do."

During this period, when I felt anxiety, I would counter my emotions with giving thanks. I began praising and thanking God for the victory, not because I felt like it, but I needed to protect my sanity. When the internal battle was too difficult, my husband and friends helped strengthen me. But deep down inside, I knew my peace of mind had to come from God. No human being could give me that inner peace. He was the only one that could provide victory. Unfailingly, God calmed my soul time and time again. Faith would replace fear and anticipation replaced dread.

It was a long battle. After a year and a half, my lawyer called and said, "It doesn't look promising. Since your insurance was only $50,000, I'm not confident we are going to win. The court date is set for ten days from now." I could tell by the tone in his voice that my one advocate was bailing out on me.

As I hung up the phone I felt panic and pictured myself vulnerable in front of an unmerciful judge. I quickly called my mom to see if she would babysit the kids while I went to court. Out of sheer willpower, I began praying and thanking God. Suddenly, I felt impressed to call a friend who had recently mentioned she knew a good Christian lawyer that might also help represent me.

Just days before the court date, I met with this new lawyer free of charge. Much to our surprise, when the woman suing me saw there was another lawyer involved, she immediately dropped the case. She settled for an amount less than our insurance company originally agreed to pay her. It was all over. The court date was cancelled, and we didn't have to pay one penny out of pocket. God had been my advocate. Now I finally obtained the promise I had been thanking Him for. It was time to celebrate. I saw the fulfillment of Hebrews 10:36. "For you have need of endurance, so that after you have done the will of God, you may receive the promise…."

He Delivers Us

There is a narrative I love in the Old Testament about a man named Jehoshaphat who understood how to press through life's difficulty with praise and thanksgiving. The greatest battle that this king ever faced was when the people of Moab and Amnon came against him. Immediately he cried out to God and prayed, "For we have no power against this great multitude that is coming against us; nor do we know what to do, but our eyes are upon You" (2 Chron. 20:12b). Jehoshaphat's battle was no different than ours, but he knew the One that could help him.

In verse 19 it says the inhabitants of Jerusalem started worshiping and praising God "with voices loud and high." They sang, "Praise the Lord, For His mercy endures forever" (2 Chron. 20:21b). And while they were praising, God sent power from heaven to defeat their enemies, bringing complete victory.

I'm sure that while I was praising God in the middle of my lawsuit battle, God sent me power from heaven to help deliver me from my enemies. Praise seems to rally the hosts of heaven.

II Chronicles doesn't ignore Jehoshaphat's humanity. The third verse in this chapter says, "And Jehoshaphat feared, and set himself to seek the Lord, and proclaimed a fast throughout all Judah." It doesn't say he felt complete peace. But he pressed through those negative feelings and sought after God. Because of his step of obedience, he gave birth to a great victory for all of Israel. Praise and thanksgiving carried him to the other side, and it will carry us all through to victory. If only we could see what happens in the heavenly realm when we praise Him—the angels taking the offense against the demonic forces with clashing swords and shields. I'm sure it would be a sight to behold.

God is always teaching His children new lessons along the way. Now that the class of "thanksgiving and praise" was underway, I was about to be enrolled in some new learning. One night in a dream, I took my seat at a desk at the back of a large classroom. I noticed the teacher called the class to attention. When I woke up, I knew that the Lord was revealing to me that He was about to teach me something new.

Chapter Five

Shut Out the Discouragers

U PS transferred Mike to their Tualatin hub, so we moved to Salem, Oregon, to be closer to family. We found a small evangelical church within walking distance from our home. Several fir trees towered high into the sky and bunches of pink petunias and yellow daffodils were sprinkled near the building. When we pulled into the newly blacktopped parking lot, I could smell the fresh bark dust all around. Some of the patron saints cared for the property as if it were their own. It was here that we became close friends with a lady that had the gift of faith stronger than anyone I had known. Our relationship with her stretched me beyond what I considered comfortable. And if there was a person who soon would be facing insurmountable odds, it was her.

Our new church was family-centered with an inviting kids program for our elementary-aged children. I remember dropping Candace, our youngest, off in Sunday school, and her teacher would immediately scoop her into her lap. Our pastor was a father of the faith and open to the gifts of the Spirit. He was tall in stature and carried an authority that commanded respect. Eventually, the Holy Spirit drew us to commit to this group of people.

Several months later the announcement was made. Our pastor was retiring. Before long, the values and practices of the church shifted. Prayer was still available for the sick, but there was no more expectation that they would actually get healed.

The story I'm about to tell you is of one heroic woman who went against the grain of religion and modeled to me a dynamic faith that saw miraculous results. But what was even more significant was she had extreme opposition.

One Sunday morning the service was nearing the end, and the pianist was playing softly as the pastor waited for people to come forward to the altar to receive prayer. Then, like clockwork, Sue steadied her husband, Ron, on the red-carpeted aisle like she did every Sunday. Because of Ron's brain tumor, he was having difficulty walking, so he leaned up against his wife. She was practically dragging him down the aisle. Fortunately she was a physically strong woman. Many of the parishioners glared at her, and I could almost feel them thinking, *How could she get his hopes up like this? What if God doesn't heal him? She is making a fool out of them both.* Some of the people came to her to warn her of just that. This church had not seen many healings for some time now, let alone miracles.

I remember the day that Sue phoned me and asked if Mike and I would stand in faith with them for Ron's healing. She had complete confidence that God would heal him no matter how long it took. There was absolutely no doubt in her voice, even when the circumstances looked bleak. I didn't feel my faith was as strong, but I answered, "Sure, we will agree with you for his healing." We only spoke words of faith for him, both to others and in prayer. But inwardly I wrestled with doubt.

The date for surgery finally arrived. Surely the doctor would remove the entire tumor and everything would be fine.

Later that day, Sue called and said, "Because of the location of the tumor, it couldn't be removed. The doctors aren't giving him much hope, but I know God will heal him."

Ron continued to deteriorate and needed more and more care. Eventually he couldn't turn over in bed on his own, and Sue had to wake up every two hours during the night and turn him over to the other side. I wondered how she was going to keep going with so little sleep.

The next time I saw Sue, her eyes looked tired and swollen from the sleepless nights, but she kept pushing ahead. Ron's eyesight was dimming, his speech was slurred, and his hands were shaking. The doctor said he would lose his sight altogether. Before he regressed too much, we had them over for dinner one night, and Ron was shaking so hard that I thought the glasses might spill over. We continued to declare that God was his healer, but there weren't any signs that this was true.

One evening, Sue held a birthday party for Ron in the church fellowship hall. Posters decorated the walls with healing Scriptures and promises. Looking at Sue, you couldn't tell she was going through any difficulty. Her face beamed as she served the punch.

The people continued to criticize her, saying, "She's just setting her husband up for disappointment." But with all the opposition, I never heard her say a word of doubt. God gave her a supernatural gift of faith. She knew beyond all doubt that God would heal him.

In the beginning, there was no change whatsoever; all she had to hold on to was her faith in the Word of God. Promises from the Bible were taped to her bathroom mirror and all around her home. Her eyes would glance at the index cards placed on her car's dashboard as she listened to faith messages on tape. Some Sunday evenings she attended a small Pentecostal church that inspired and encouraged her. Those meetings strengthened her spirit and gave her more fuel to face the challenges that presented themselves the next week. Her mind was being renewed on the truth from morning to night. She hung on to the prophetic words that the Lord had already spoken (1 Tim. 1:18). She didn't let the negativity from the people at church affect her but rather surrounded herself with the truth.

Finally, months later, upon examination, the doctor said, "The tumor has shrunk just a small amount in size! I can't explain it!" At first the change was barely noticeable, but it was uplifting to see some evidence that prayer was working. Every time he was examined, the tumor got smaller. However, the doctor said that Ron would never be able to drive again and his eyesight would not improve. Sue prayed the opposite.

Several months later, the tumor completely disappeared. His eyesight returned to normal, and he drove his car again for the first time. I remember the day she told me that Ron was returning to work. The critical words from the church people didn't come to pass. She made a decision to hold on to the Word and close her ears to the opposition.

Sue's faith resembled the faith I read about in Scripture. And I realized then more than ever that the people I associated with would eventually influence my life for the good or for bad. I would do the same for them. If Sue would have surrounded herself with negative people and took their words to heart, I'm sure it would have been more difficult to hang on to God's Word.

Good Friends Make All the Difference

Can you relate to the toughness of staying positive when you're surrounded by negativity? If you try to protect your mind from discouragement, but the people around you are constantly negative, it's easy to eventually get worn down. Before long you can pick up on their attitudes and begin to sound similar to them. Paul tells us to "not be deceived: Evil company corrupts good habits" (1 Cor. 15:33). But of course the opposite is true when you become a team player with a person of good character. Your faith grows and things that once seemed impossible become more possible.

Just so that I'm not misunderstood, I'm not discouraging evangelism. Reaching out and loving the pre-Christian is part of our commission. I'm making reference to the close-knit soul ties that we form in the body of Christ, the people we choose to connect with deeply. These are the people we come into alliance with.

In the previous chapter, I shared that King Jehoshaphat followed after God and let the high praises of God defeat his enemies. But have you read about the end of his life? In order to make ships go more easily to Tarshish, he allied himself with Ahaziah, king of Israel, who was a wicked man. A prophet then prophesied over Jehoshaphat and said, "'Because you have allied yourself with Ahaziah, the Lord has destroyed your works.' Then the ships were wrecked, so that they were not able to go to Tarshish" (2 Chron. 20:37b). I didn't realize that God took alliances that seriously.

One day, I opened up a book by Rick Joyner titled, *A Prophetic Vision for the 21*st *Century.* Rick lists five characteristics of achievers—people who achieve great things in their lives. One of them is "They do not associate with 'problem-oriented people', but with 'solution-oriented people.'"[ii] I remember back in our twenties when we were on staff at the Yorba Linda Vineyard, all the home group leaders were advised to encourage their groups to stay away from fellowshipping around problems. That was good advice for groups as well as for one-on-one relationships. It's beneficial to let our words bring edification to others around us and to pick our close friends carefully.

I was beginning to realize that I needed cheerleaders in my inner circle, people who would stand with me when I felt weak, people who believed in me despite my imperfections, and more importantly, people of faith who believed in God's ability to perform His Word.

Attack on the Inside

Discouragement doesn't always attack from the outside. As I discussed earlier, there's the opposition that can internally assault the mind. Protecting the mind from these negative onslaughts is just as important as keeping out the wrong alliances. Learning to encourage oneself in the Lord and keep the mind free from negative thoughts protects us from the thief who loves to steal faith and hope. The Bible is bursting with promises to stand on when opposition strikes. A great verse to declare when facing inner turmoil is "Now thanks be to God who always leads us in triumph in Christ" (2 Cor. 2:14a).

Chapter Six

Expecting the Supernatural

Not Your Everyday Story

A few months after Ron's healing, we were drawn to a new church back in the quaint town of Albany, Oregon, where we used to live. A strong healing anointing attracted us to the Saturday night services. Our kids didn't mind the thirty-minute drive south because we always stopped for Burger King hamburgers on the way home.

After we had attended this church for about a year, my mom and sister were each admitted to the hospital the same week to have surgeries; one was on the fourth floor and one on the second. Mike and I decided to visit them with our elementary-age children. It was Saturday and our family first enjoyed a big pancake breakfast together. Then I ran to get dressed and scurried out to our garage to grab some mail out of the small mailbox. This box was located by the garage door directly behind our car. Standing there, I paused to skim through a letter and lost track of time.

Mike was completely unaware that I was behind the station wagon and led the kids out to the car. I didn't hear him start the engine. Suddenly, the vehicle backed up right on top of my left ankle. I pounded frantically on the back car window and screamed at the top of my lungs. Our children started to yell at their dad, feeling traumatized at the sight of my panicked face.

My mouth was open so wide they could see my tonsils. Mike, trying not to shatter my foot, was slowly inching forward, but so gradually that it seemed like it was happening in slow motion.

When my foot was finally released from the weight of the car, we surveyed the damage. The ankle was swelling, the skin turning purple, and I felt searing pain when I put pressure on my foot. Not knowing if I had broken a bone, we took a detour to the ER instead of going straight to visit our relatives on the upper floors.

After studying the X-rays, the doctor said, "Fortunately, there is no fracture, but it will take time to heal." The nurse assisted me into a wheelchair so I could visit my mom and sister. But the excitement didn't end there.

That night we drove to our church. After I got over the shock of being run over, I was expectant that God was going to heal me.

When we arrived, I limped over to our pastor and his wife and asked for prayer. The instant they touched my foot, I felt extreme heat that lasted for minutes. The pain disappeared, and when I stood up, I felt no symptoms at all. I jumped up and down and—still no pain. I lifted my hands to praise God and continued to thank Him for my healing. Mike, feeling terrible that it had happened, was rejoicing with me. With the pain gone, I found the whole accident rather hilarious.

All the bruising and swelling disappeared within the next few days. Not only did I experience an instantaneous healing, but it seemed like almost everyone I prayed for in that season was healed as well.

Air-Lifted from Shasta Lake

Four years later, I folded my last bit of laundry while the kids played outside. I ran to grab the phone that was ringing in the kitchen. My brother Randy's voice sounded out of breath as he said, "Pray for Brandon; he drowned in Shasta Lake and has been air-lifted to the hospital. We'll call when we know more. Tell people to pray." My brother hung up before I could ask questions. My adrenalin went on high alert!

My dear sister's baby, Brandon, had just turned four, a darling little curly-haired boy. I had seen the miraculous power of God before, and although I could feel the tension in my body, I began declaring the promises of God. I called loved ones and prayer chains to pray for a miracle as my children stood nearby. I told my kids, "Brandon drowned, but he will be healed." My youngest daughter, Candace, felt peace as she thought, *Yeah, definitely, God will heal him.*

My brother and sister's families had just arrived at Lake Shasta for vacation in California. It was frustrating for me to be so far away in Oregon, but we prayed continually as we waited for more word. The next call brought a bit more information. A stranger spotted Brandon's little body floating in the lake. His initial thought was, *This boy is messing around and needs to move out of the way of my boat.* But when the man drew closer and noticed the boy was motionless and face down in the water, he scooped him up and yelled, "Whose kid is this? Someone get this dead baby out of my arms!" It all happened so fast. How had he disappeared from view?

A lady dashed over to try CPR on his lifeless body while my brother Randy held Brandon's feet and prayed for a miracle. Suddenly, Brandon started to breathe and let out a strange cry. But he was still comatose when the helicopter landed.

"He probably won't make it, but if he does, he will be brain-dead," the doctor told my sister, Crystal, as she stared at her son. Even though he was unresponsive, she continued to talk to him. "Brandon, we'll get you a Batman movie when we get home." There was no reply. The hours dragged on.

After twenty-four hours of waiting and praying, suddenly Brandon muttered, "Let's go home and get the Batman movie." What? It was like someone hit the "on" button and everything was back to normal. Crystal signaled for the nurse. His brain function and all tests showed there were no negative effects from the drowning.

God once again demonstrated His great power. We thanked and praised the Lord for showing us there's nothing impossible with God (Luke 1:37).

But the crazy thing is, even after witnessing the amazing miracles up to this point in my life, sometimes I battled fears and frustration like many others. However, the time spent listening to lies and fears was becoming less and less.

Tools to Help Stay Expectant

I've shared stories about how God led me to various tools from Scripture that brought strength to my soul as I faced challenges. The following is a list that I hope will benefit you. At times, in the middle of warfare, I've needed to use all of them. As you read, maybe you're in the middle of a crisis right now. Or possibly you're just feeling discouraged, worried, or frustrated. Before you go on, I invite you to take some time to encourage yourself in the Lord.

Tools That Bring Strength and Courage

- Praise and worship the Lord.
- Offer thanksgiving for all He has done in the past, what He is going to do, and for who He is.
- Renew your mind. Check what thoughts are being allowed to stay; get rid of the harmful, toxic ones.
- Stand on the promises of God, declaring them out loud. Begin to memorize promises from Scripture that you can use as weapons against the enemy.
- If you've been given prophetic words for your future, declare them into the atmosphere. Maybe there are things God has spoken directly into your spirit; speak them out and begin thanking the Lord for His ability to perform what He said He will do (1 Tim. 1:18).
- Turn to Scripture and begin reading. Bill Johnson, from Bethel Church, often says that sometimes he reads through the Psalms until he begins to hear God speak.[iii]

- Turn to the Lord in prayer; call on His name for help.
- If you have a spiritual prayer language, pray out loud in tongues; this will help your spirit to connect with the Spirit of God, bypassing your mind which may be trying to analyze the situation. Freedom and hope will eventually begin to take hold. And sometimes the Lord will download new strategies.
- Call or text a brother or sister and ask them to stand in agreement with you for your breakthrough.
- Get rid of unforgiveness.
- Don't lose your sense of humor; laughter is good medicine.
- Have an obedient heart.
- Quiet your spirit and wait in silence for the peace of God to fill you. Stay in a place of rest and trust.

Standing on the Word

Just as Brandon held fast to his mother's promise even in his subconscious, we can cling to the promises of God. When he was in a coma, all he heard was, "When you get well, we'll go get a Batman movie," and he trusted his mother's word to make it happen. We can believe God will do what He says because of the faithful God that He is. He is always true to His Word. Even if we're asleep spiritually, His voice can awaken our spirits to life. When we make Him big in our eyes, anticipation grows. While focusing on His great ability, the problems become smaller, and His supernatural power seems more likely to happen.

The Father of the Faith

One man that passed God's tests of faith was Abraham. We call him the Great Father of the Faith because he knew what it was like to keep believing God's Word when it was humanly impossible for breakthrough. In talking about Abraham, Paul says, "He did not waver at the promise of God through unbelief, but was strengthened in faith, giving glory to God, and being fully convinced that what He had promised He was also able to perform" (Rom. 4:20-21).

Have you thought about how many months Sarah went through her monthly cycle and still no pregnancy? On top of that, I'm sure that facing menopause was a big disappointment. And then after all those years of waiting, how many women want to give birth at ninety? Also, she had to let go of her desire to be a young mother as well as a grandmother. But the supernatural breakthrough of the promised son came to pass in Abraham and Sarah's life—it came in God's timing and in God's way.

Touch from Heaven

Maybe you need a supernatural healing today. If so, I invite the anointing of Jehovah Rapha, the Healer, to shine His light throughout your body. I bless you with His healing power and freedom from pain in Jesus' precious name. I pray that your faith in Christ, who performs the impossible, will soar higher than ever before. "[He] is able to do exceedingly abundantly above all that we ask or think, according to the power that works in us" (Eph. 3:20).

If you are reading this and you don't have a relationship with the Son of God, Jesus Christ, I invite you to experience the greatest supernatural miracle on earth. He is ready to transform all your emptiness into rich hope and purpose and give you eternal life. And it's free. You can receive this gift by faith in Jesus Christ's finished work on the cross. He not only paid for your physical healing, but even more importantly, He paid for your salvation from sin. Psalm 103 says, "Bless the Lord, O my soul, And forget not all His benefits: Who forgives all your iniquities, Who heals all your diseases" (Ps. 103:2-3). Today can be the day you surrender your life to the Creator who formed you in your mother's womb—the one who knows you better than you know yourself. Today can be your first day of living a supernatural life.

Chapter Seven

Give Up? What For?

My Violin (Two Years Later)

O ur kids entered junior high and high school. One hot
August Saturday afternoon, our family and several friends
enjoyed a picnic at the crowded Foster Lake in Sweet Home,
Oregon. The smell of hamburgers barbequing and the sound
of children laughing and splashing water filled the summer air
while some of us sat on lawn chairs with our feet soaking in
the lake to keep cool. Our friends had invited a new family to
join us, and the gentleman strolled over to meet me. After the
introductions, he said, "You know, I believe the Lord wants
to bring healing to your left hand. What's wrong with your
hand?" He knew nothing about my accident. Again, sparks
of anticipation flickered at the possibility. After he prayed,
although my nerve and hand weren't healed yet, something new
was birthed inside of me.

On the way home, I found myself thinking, *Lord, I surrender
to You. As I wait for a miracle, I will use my limited ability for
Your glory.*

At home later that evening, I anxiously headed toward my
violin. The instrument looked beautiful as I lifted it out of its
dusty case. I reflected back to the scene of the accident and
felt thankful that all my violin students had cancelled lessons
that day. Because they did, this instrument remained safely at

home while I had carted only my guitar in the trunk of my car. At the scene, my acoustic guitar was shredded into sawdust, leaving only the six mangled strings and the wooden signature piece that said Yamaha. Fortunately, my violin hadn't suffered the same fate.

My mind traveled back to my sixteenth birthday when Dad surprised me with this gift packaged in a nice hard-shelled case. I had always loved the deep, rich tone.

I lifted the instrument to my chin to sweep the strings with the bow and played a few melodies by ear. The frustration at the inability to use all my fingers was still there; but I felt the deep desire to play, and I enjoyed making the musical sound unique to this instrument.

Mike and the kids gathered around to listen. Up to this time, our children had only heard me play once or twice before. Now as teenagers, their encouragement cheered me on to play more. Eventually our daughter Shannon got out her guitar, and Jason his drum set, and we began to worship together.

The three of us started to lead worship in home groups and gatherings. I would always invite the Holy Spirit to help my fingers play the notes.

People laid hands on me and prayed for healing often in the following days and years, and *hope* became my companion. I had watched God heal many people and realized how much He loves to restore what's been broken. But even more than desiring to experience the miracle on my nerve, I longed to know God on a deeper level and fall more in love with the Healer. After all, He is so many things to me—my Shepherd, my Redeemer, Provider, Healer, Deliverer, and Enduring Friend! More and more He filled the empty places in my heart. Over the years, my identity had shifted from my performance to the security of being a daughter of the Most High. My trust was in His never-ending faithfulness.

Remembering the immersion of the love of God while recuperating in the hospital and the many times I had already experienced His fulfilling presence, I spent hours just worshiping Him. And now, for the first time, I worshiped on my violin.

One of the first times I played violin on a worship team, a prophetic gentleman came up to me and said, "Play the sounds you hear in heaven. Listen with your spiritual ears and play what you hear." I wanted to say, "You don't understand; I'm not able to play a lot of what I hear." I wanted to tell him all about the accident, but I said nothing.

One night, while playing on a worship team, the leader pointed to me to improvise a solo. My immediate thought was, *You're kidding, aren't you?* But I stepped out. What followed was a surprise to me; notes and double-stops I couldn't do in the natural were easily flowing. God anointed me to play supernaturally that night.

Upon returning home, in the quiet of my bedroom, I lifted my instrument out of the case to repeat the performance. The notes didn't flow as before. It felt like Cinderella at midnight. Even though I had begun my faith journey, I felt disappointed.

I Asked God a Question

Later, I asked the Lord a question I had never asked Him in all these years. "How do You feel about my severed nerve from the accident?" Even though I understood much more of the goodness of God, I assumed that possibly He allowed this loss because the violin was too important to me when I was young or maybe I wasn't passionate enough about God. Why did I still have this wrong impression of God deep down in my soul? Why did I still think that maybe if I had been more perfect, the accident wouldn't have happened?

After I asked the question, I heard in my spirit, *I was very sad I didn't hear you play violin for those many years. Don't ever think I didn't love you. I have loved you more than you could ever know. And you didn't lose any of the anointing I have given you. The anointing on your life will increase. I am replacing your mourning with joy. Receive more of my joy. I have much more for you.*

As I sat alone meditating on what I just heard, I thought about how God was using my playing to minister to people even now in my weakness. I considered the truth that His joy and love is continually overshadowing me in spite of all my frailty. At that moment I chose to change my wrong belief about God and replace it with the truth that He is and always has been *for* me.

Just like an earthly father would not give his son a disease or an accident to teach him a lesson, God was not the one that struck me with this destruction. But there is an enemy that seeks to kill, steal, and destroy. And there is evil and sin present in this world that causes a lot of chaos and pain. God is and always has been the Restorer of the broken, the Healer of our bodies and souls, and the Redeemer from the curse of the law.

I knew I did not have all the answers as to why this or any other destructive thing would happen. But Psalm 103:4 says, "[He] redeems [my] life from destruction, [He] crowns [me] with lovingkindness and tender mercies." I could continue to wait with expectation. I could wait for my healing in anticipation of His goodness in all areas of my life. I sat in stillness as I reflected on His loving nature.

How Long Have You Waited?

So many things in life seem to take a long time. But fortunately, when God brings breakthrough and change, it often comes suddenly. Maybe God made you a promise but you've waited and waited. You're not alone. The Bible is filled with true accounts of people just like us that patiently endured for months, years, and even decades for breakthrough. These people chose to be overcomers.

Noah was a man that found favor with God and walked closely with Him. In fact, he was the only person in his day that pleased God—talk about feeling alone. Because of man's wickedness on the earth, the Lord told Noah that he was going to destroy all flesh. The account in Genesis says that the people in Noah's day were so wicked that every thought they had was continually evil (Gen. 6:5). They had no good thoughts. Obviously, Noah wasn't going to get encouragement from his neighbors. He couldn't just go attend an uplifting church service. God was his only encourager. Then the Lord made a special covenant with Noah that he and his family would be spared the upcoming disaster. But this protection wasn't going to come easily. Noah was given an assignment with detailed instructions on how to build an enormous ark.

The Bible isn't clear about how long it took to build this huge boat. Many say it was 120 years because of Genesis 6:3. But we do know that Noah was 500 years old when he had his first son in Genesis 5:32, and he was 600 when the floodwaters came upon the earth (Gen. 7:6). Since the boat was so large, it probably took quite a few years to build even with the help of his sons. The ark's dimensions were approximately 450 feet by 75 feet wide by 45 feet high.

So Noah's story in a nutshell is: Noah received a promise from God. Next, he needed endurance to complete the difficult task of building and loading up the ark. Eventually, he and his sons experienced deliverance and began their new adventure. There is no account of his feelings throughout this process. But being a human being, there is little doubt that he felt like giving up from time to time. I'm sure he was troubled when he thought about his friends and relatives that resisted God. He may have felt weary from the huge assignment. But just like us, he focused his attention on the promise ahead and the task at hand.

There are others in the Bible that refused to give up. Hannah waited for a son while her husband's other wife, Peninnah, bore child after child. Elizabeth, Mary's cousin, waited to become pregnant with John the Baptist. And the apostle Paul suffered much opposition and persecution in his life but continued to believe God to the end. Their life stories are written to keep us strengthened as we all live out our personal stories.

Too often, people stop praying for breakthrough right before God is ready to bring the manifestation of His kingdom down to earth. In 2 Peter 1:6–8, Peter mentions the character quality of *perseverance* when he lists the ingredients needed in order to be fruitful. In a fast-food, high-tech society, perseverance is not popular. But in order to obtain the promises and come into maturity in Christ, we need this quality. It's what helps us to become overcomers. The enemy would love nothing more than to see Christians get frustrated and throw in the towel. He seems to know just the right buttons to press to tempt us into discouragement. But the devil presents illusions because he's a liar. And no matter what things look like or feel like, God's promises are true.

Oddly enough, I think one of the biggest targets of the enemy is to get Christians bored. It's not always the traumatic trials that tempt a person into depression; it's more often the mundane. Somehow, after a season of life as usual, it's easy to feel trapped into thinking things will never change.

If you've had one discouragement after another, the weariness of battle begs to settle in. Often the oppression can feel the greatest in the evening hours, in the darkness of the night. There can be a temptation to begin to speak out words of hopelessness and defeat, causing discouragement to go even deeper. Somehow, the morning light often brings new hope. So when the urge to give up begins to weigh heavy on the heart, it's time to see God for who He really is and speak out what He says is true in His Word. For Christ is faithful even in the dark night of the soul. Paul says in 2 Timothy, "And the Lord will deliver me from every evil work and preserve me for His heavenly kingdom. To Him be glory forever and ever. Amen!" (2 Tim. 4:18).

God wants to meet our every need. There are enemies of our souls, but God isn't one of them. The apostle Paul said, "If God is for us, who can be against us?" (Rom. 8:31b). So let's be encouraged today to allow the patience and longsuffering of Christ to work in us until we see the fulfillment of His promises. And along with David we can say:

> "I will lift up my eyes to the hills
> From whence comes my help?
> My help comes from the Lord,
> Who made heaven and earth" (Ps. 121:1).

Was It a Waste?

Not long after I started to play the violin again, my sister-in-law invited the kids and me to visit a friend who was in the late stages of cancer. Mike and I had seen people healed of cancer, and I was confident she would be another.

This woman was full of faith and discussed plans for her future and the future of her three young children. She continually confessed that she already had her healing, and her countenance radiated more than I'd ever seen on one so sick. I'm sure there were many days that she endured lots of pain and discouragement, but there was fortitude in her voice that was obviously from God.

A couple of weeks later, we got a phone call and were shocked to hear that she suddenly passed away. I could imagine some people saying, "What a waste. She hung on for nothing." After I got over the shock of her passing, a light turned on in my head. The faith that sustained this woman and the faith-filled prayers of her companions was not a wasted faith. She was able to meet her Master without all the unbelief and fear that accompanies so many to eternity. She never gave up hope, even to the end. I felt the Father's pleasure as I contemplated the way she trusted God, as a little child trusts her father.

I remembered the verse in Hebrews 11:13 that says, "These all died in faith, not having received the promises, but having seen them afar off were assured of them, embraced them and confessed that they were strangers and pilgrims on the earth." I read that Abraham and many other people of faith all throughout history received part of their promises in this life, but hung on until the end. They met the Savior with a heart of expectancy and believed that the provision of God was greater than the obstacles they faced. They believed that what God said in His

Word, He was able to perform. They understood that God is looking for men and women of faith, and He's pleased when He finds faith on the earth (Luke 18:8).

Give Up?

One afternoon a few months later, I listened to a motivational message from a familiar pastor on the radio. He was telling a story about a heroic woman who fought against the odds to accomplish a feat no other woman had ever performed, swimming across the English Channel. This story brought such encouragement to me that I drove to the library to check out a book on her life. Once in the car, I rolled down my window to let in the fresh air as I began reading her story. Elizabeth Kimmel describes the following story:

Once Gertrude Ederle had already swum for miles, the violent seas began to swell to monstrous-sized waves and her trainer begged her to stop swimming. She yelled back, "What for?"[iv] and continued to press through. This heroic nineteen-year-old swam with determination to finish all the way to the beach at Kingsdown, England. She became the first woman to swim the English Channel, twenty-one miles across. And since much of the time she was swimming against the current, it became a thirty-five mile feat. The waters were icy cold and inhabited by jellyfish, Portuguese man-of-wars, and occasionally a shark, but Ederle wasn't deterred and went all the way across the channel to the finish.

I put the book down and reflected about the many times that I've faced insurmountable odds and heard the enemy chant, "Give up, give up." Often the obstacles seemed like jellyfish, sharks, or monstrous-sized waves, but God gave me the courage to yell back, "What for?" God was again speaking the familiar theme of perseverance into my spirit.

Graveyard Shift Again?

Just as God had been teaching me about endurance in my life, it had now been fifteen years since my husband began to work at United Parcel Service. Many of those years he had been trying to get out. The long hours were taxing him in every area. The final straw fell when his boss assigned him to the graveyard shift—again!

Mike's working day was thirteen to fifteen hours long and was much harder when working nights. He came home, slept for three hours, and then sped off to our daughter's high school basketball games. I don't think he missed one. Then returning home, he would eat, sleep for another two or three hours before heading back to work only to begin the cycle all over again.

Although family was a huge priority to Mike, the long hours and stress were taking a toll on our marriage and family. The prayer I began praying for Mike every day was:

"May the Lord answer you in the day of trouble;
May the name of the God of Jacob defend you;

> May He send you help from the sanctuary,
> And strengthen you out of Zion;
> May He remember all your offerings, And
> accept your burnt sacrifice. Selah
> May He grant you according to your heart's desire,
> And fulfill all your purpose" (Ps. 20:1–4).

One day, Mike noticed a friend at the UPS parking lot. She walked over to him and prophesied, "Mike, I believe God is going to give you a tailor-made job." He couldn't wait to come home and tell me the good news. We both thought it would happen overnight.

One year later, sixteen years after he began working for the company, God blessed him with the perfect job as a vice principal and dean at a private school. His whole face smiled on his yearbook picture.

It's Not Time to Quit

During those sixteen years, there were many days that it seemed to Mike that he was just wasting away, moving in the opposite direction of his destiny. But God knew that the years of management were training him for leadership in school administration. Mike tried to leave, but God wouldn't let him.

There were days, maybe a little like Joseph, when he felt he was in a prison. Everything inside his being shouted out, "I can't go through this anymore!" But eventually God answered the prayer of Psalm 20 and gave Mike his heart's desire. He walked through the open door of his new season feeling like a free man.

Maybe some of you can relate to Mike's story. Have you ever felt trapped and wanted to quit something so badly but later found out that God was in it? It wasn't the enemy after all. And the best choice was to hang on and trust God to bring you through? If Mike would have forced his way out of the company prematurely, he wouldn't have received all of his training. Who knows, maybe that would have triggered another several laps around the mountain of learning before the doors opened to the new season of destiny.

Perseverance is needed in so many areas of life, not only in long battles at work but in financial struggles, relationships, physical sickness, conflicts, and potentially any arena. Our flesh wants the gratification now, and we want to understand the complexities now. But someone once said that life isn't a sprint, it's a marathon. And often the temptation to give up is greatest just before the finish line.

Chapter Eight

Victory Seldom Comes Without a Battle

The Move

M ike enjoyed five fulfilling years at the private school in Salem. I joined him on staff to teach band and worship team. The fifth year we were there, God visited a twenty-year-old dorm parent who sparked the flames of a revival, and the fire began to sweep across the campus. It all started on April 16. The school year was almost over. The dorm parent described his spiritual encounter with the school administration before he began sharing with the high school students. High school kids spread the excitement to the junior high. Students that had never had a relationship with Christ were spiritually awakened. Even the countenances of many of them were transformed. Sometimes, when I would glance at a student, I did a double take and asked myself, *Is that the same person?* Mike and I couldn't wait to go to school every day. Right in the middle of all the excitement, I had a dream.

I woke up one morning reaching for my journal to write down the vivid scenes. I didn't want to forget the brilliant colors and descriptive details. In the dream, I was walking through an older home trying to decide if I wanted to buy it. Holding on to a massive wooden handrail, I slowly walked upstairs and then back down, peering into each room. I noticed the colors of the

Victorian furnishings and expensive wall hangings. The realtor then told me the cost of the home, and I said, "No, that's too expensive. I can't afford that!"

Fully awake, I sat in bed thinking about the dream. I wondered if God was going to ask me to do something that would cost me a lot.

A month later, the phone rang while I was vacuuming. I caught the end of the message and heard, "Mike, we received your résumé, and we're interested in having you come down to our school in Redding for an interview." What? I had no idea that Mike applied for a principal position in Redding, and I didn't want to move to California.

When Mike got home, he assured me that we wouldn't be making any decision without my consensus. He said, "I noticed this job opening and simply sent a résumé out of curiosity." Then he added, "I didn't take it seriously." Now that they were asking for an interview, he was nearly as surprised as I was.

It all happened so fast. About three months later, Mike led the caravan south as he drove the large moving truck towing Candace's pickup. Behind him, our daughter Shannon and her boyfriend, Rodney, drove our van pulling the tent trailer while Candace and I took up the rear with the Toyota Camry.

Once everything was unloaded, we tearfully sent Shannon and Rodney back to Salem on the Amtrak train. My mind began to reflect on all that had transpired the last couple of days as I watched their train disappear. Two days earlier, we had said our good-byes to our son, Jason, our loving parents, siblings, and many dear friends that helped us move. Jason drove up to spend that last night with us before we moved away. I remember he said, "You really are moving away, aren't you, Mom?" Even though he was about twenty-five and living on his own, it was heart-wrenching for a mother to hear those words. I hoped that the kids understood that we didn't want to leave them, but God was calling us away.

The next day, we moved everything out of our house except Shannon's bedroom furniture. We hadn't sold our home yet, so Shannon, age twenty-three, was going to continue to live in that empty house alone for a while. I couldn't even wrap my mind around that. Fortunately, our youngest daughter, Candace, was moving to Redding with us. But I was beginning to feel the cost of the call.

I loved every bit of being a mother from the day they were born. Family was a priority. Now I spent days shedding tears in anticipation of the move and more tears once we were settled. But I knew beyond all doubt that we were being obedient.

The Lord confirmed in several ways that this was His will. First, most of our friends and family knew in their hearts that we were to go. Also, deep in my spirit, I felt anticipation and peace about the move; He led Mike and me by His still, small voice. Finally, the Lord downloaded several dreams that He was directing us to make this change. And I understood that obedience was key to living a life expecting the goodness of God.

Once we were settled in Redding, the bright California sun and the adventure of getting to know a new city made the move a bit easier. I knew in my spirit that God would bring fruit and victory after this emotional battle.

Bike Accident

Nine months later, early in the morning, the phone rang. By the time I got it, the person had hung up. It was my soon-to-be son-in-law, Rodney. The message said, "Shannon's been in an accident. It looks like she's okay, but I'm headed to the hospital now." I could tell he didn't want to worry me and stayed as positive as he could. But I could hardly breathe as I listened to the message a couple of times. I was still in my bathrobe, my Bible opened on my bed from my morning reading. It was dark outside, and my small lamp was the only light on in my bedroom.

The day was May 12, exactly two months before our daughter was to marry Rodney Smith, a handsome man we had all grown to love. And now here we were, seven hours away from the hospital waiting for more word.

I returned Rodney's call but got no answer, as he was probably on his way to the hospital. I prayed, *Oh God, I speak the blood of Jesus and the power of Your resurrection over*

Shannon right now. Oh Lord, hear my prayer. I give You praise for Your power. I believe for a miracle. Your Word says, "By [Your] stripes [she is] healed" (Isa. 53:5).

I paced the floor as I waited for Rod's call. The minutes seemed like hours, but soon I heard his voice on the line. "Shannon was in a bike accident," he began, "but she's okay. There's a gash on her forehead, and her shoulder is possibly dislocated. I guess she was riding her bike to work when she and a car collided. The impact threw her into the air before her head hit the windshield. She wasn't wearing a helmet, but she seems to be doing pretty well in the ER. My parents are there with her now." After a few more words, we hung up and I called Mike. This was going to be hard news for him to receive on his birthday.

I was so relieved that she was alive, but I was concerned about the gash on her forehead. *How big was it, anyway? And how bad was her shoulder injury?* I wondered how she was doing emotionally, but I tried not to let my imagination go wild. With her wedding eight weeks away, we needed a quick recovery.

A few hours after the accident, I finally reached Shannon in the hospital. She answered right away, but I had difficulty talking through my tears and finally had to hang up. I thought, *That did not go well. I need to encourage her; I'll try again.* I called back, trying to keep myself composed and relay the message I intended to give her the first time. I said, "Don't worry, Shannon. We will believe together for complete healing. It's going to happen."

That same day, my sister, Crystal, called and described Shannon's head injury. "The doctor wanted to just stitch her up, Cin, but I asked for a plastic surgeon," my sister began. "They listened to me, and thankfully a plastic surgeon is coming in a few hours." I replied, "Thanks so much, Sis! I'm so glad you are there with her." She continued to try to encourage me and keep me from worrying. But later I found out that she and her daughter, Brittany, had burst into tears immediately when they walked into her room and witnessed Shannon's head injury. Since the nurse still hadn't cleaned the wound, it was covered in blood.

Before long, Shannon's grandparents and other family and friends gathered at her bedside. Her soon-to-be father-in-law cracked jokes trying to keep the atmosphere lighthearted. It seemed like everyone was there except us.

My two wind ensembles from school were scheduled to perform the spring concert in a few days. Should I cancel? I had no peace to cancel, but I had trouble concentrating on my commitments.

The night of the concert, I walked up to the stage and briefly described Shannon's accident and requested their prayers. I could feel the warm concern over the audience as I told them that I was thanking the Lord and believing for her healing. Then we proceeded with the program.

The next morning, Candace and I loaded up the car for our trip to Oregon to finally see Shannon. She was staying with her soon-to-be in-laws so they could nurse her back to health.

As we drove up the driveway to Rodney's parent's home, Shannon walked toward our car. Her face was tan and beautiful, but approximately sixteen dark stitches etched a U shape around the top of her forehead. Thankfully, it looked better than I had imagined. We told her she looked beautiful and walked into the house together.

Candace and I laid hands on her head and prayed for healing several times in the next few days. Although I wrestled with doubt as I thought about the approaching wedding, we all spoke words of faith.

We didn't see her again until days before the wedding. My eyes immediately glanced at her forehead. I couldn't even notice a trace of the scar. Her wedding pictures were beautiful, and her shoulder, after therapy, was much improved. God showed His power once again.

I thanked the Lord because while He had called me and Mike away to minister to young people in Redding, God was tending to the needs of our own children.

By now our new city was feeling like home. I loved the warm summer evenings, sipping cold drinks, wearing shorts and flip flops. The days of shedding tears over the move seemed further in the past. We were beginning to see some fruit from our labor at the school. Gradually there were some students that noticeably began hungering after God. There's nothing like seeing the eyes of the youth come alive with expectation to see God move in their lives. Joy was triumphing over sadness.

To top it off, Shannon and Rodney were talking about moving down to live near us. I couldn't wait. Shannon was hired as a junior high social studies teacher at our school, and Rod sold his business in Oregon and started up his leather repair business in Redding. They moved into an apartment five minutes away.

The next couple of years were filled with lots of warm family gatherings, celebrating holidays, birthdays, and everything we could celebrate. Rodney began keeping an eye out for a husband for Candace, our unmarried daughter. At twenty-six, she was ready to tie the knot.

Broken-Down Truck

One hot summer afternoon, four years after we moved to Redding, Candace walked into the front door with frustration written all over her face. "The mechanic says I need to get rid of my truck," she said as she strolled into the kitchen, reaching for her laptop. Her 1994 Nissan pickup had been so reliable for years, but it was suffering from old age. I noticed that after a couple of hours of staring at the computer her eyes glazed over. She pointed out car after car, and each one looked like junk to me. Day after day she searched, praying and believing God to provide the vehicle she needed, but after time her eyes looked weary.

We heard about this new provision by the state for vehicles that no longer could pass the smog test but were in running order, and Candace's truck qualified for the $1,500 they were offering. That in itself was a great deal since she bought this truck five years earlier from a neighbor for only $400. And it really hadn't given any problems until now.

Soon, Candace was holding the $1,500 from her Nissan, and a family member loaned her another $1,500, but finding a car for $3,000 was not as easy as she thought. We saw cars with huge dents and cheap spray paint jobs. We rode in cars that stalled and had no shocks. Three thousand dollars doesn't give you what it used to, and it was getting difficult for our busy family of three to juggle schedules and share two cars.

For the past three years, Candace had attended ministry school; the last year she volunteered many extra hours and worked part time. In the natural, her savings was virtually empty; but God had given her supernatural provision in the past, and we knew He would do it again.

Weeks turned into months and still no car. The frustration mounted. Finally, one day she saw a classified ad for a 2003 maroon-colored Daewoo. We hadn't heard of that model of car, but the ad said it was in great running order. Since it was only forty minutes away, the three of us drove up together to see if it was as good as it looked.

After turning into a lovely neighborhood studded with tall California spruce trees, we drove up the driveway of a large Victorian home. A young, perky, middle-aged woman I'll call Nancy quickly bounced out the front door and led us to her car parked in the cul-de-sac. We enjoyed the ride and the sights of the small town as the owner explained the repairs she had done on it. Upon returning back, she looked at Candace and said, "I'll give you the car for $2,000." Not sure she heard right, Candace asked, "Two thousand?" The lady nodded yes, and Candace counted out twenty-one hundred-dollar bills to add a little tip for the ladies generous offer. We then prayed a blessing over this kind woman.

The next day, Candace and I drove to the Olive Garden for a birthday party. On the way, we noticed the engine light came on. "Oh, no, have we been taken?" I asked quietly. Candace didn't respond. After months of looking for a car, she couldn't bear to think of mechanical problems.

We tried to dismiss the car from our minds and walked into the entryway of the restaurant. Sitting on the front bench waiting was a cute, dark-haired boy that Rodney had invited. I sat down right next to him and Candace next to me. I couldn't help notice the sparks shooting back and forth as they struck up conversation. In fact, I completely forgot about the car as I noticed the chemistry mounting at the dinner table. But after the party was over, the engine light reminded us once again of the car trouble.

The following morning, Candace brought her new purchase to the mechanic and the gentleman said, "I'm sorry Candace, but this car can't pass the smog test, and it needs hundreds of dollars of repairs. I advise you to give it back to the owner, and ask her to return your money." Candace felt devastated and thought to herself, *Lord, I've waited a long time for this car, and it seemed like the right one.* She drove home and phoned Nancy.

"Candace, money isn't a problem for me," Nancy began, "so you just tell me how much the car is going to cost, and I'll send you the money." I wondered if this lady was for real or if she was playing a game.

The next day, the repairman gave the bad news. "I think I can repair everything for about $1,050. But I advise you again to give the car back to the owner; that's too much money to put into a car you just purchased, and I'm sure the owner will not give you that much money."

Candace emailed Nancy and wrote down the amount it would cost to repair everything. She heard nothing that day, but the following afternoon a truck pulled into our driveway, and a woman ran to the door. I walked out and saw it was Nancy. "Hi, would you like to come in?" I asked her. "No," she responded, "Just tell Candace that I left a package for her by your door." And she drove off.

Candace opened the package while I anxiously stood by. She counted out eleven one-hundred-dollar bills and a note that read:

Dear Candace,

I'm so sorry that the car has had all of these problems. I had no idea that it needed that much work. Enclosed is $1,100, and if you need more, I'll send it. If I overpaid you, just keep the extra for some hot chocolate.

Candace and I looked at each other in astonishment. We were witnessing a financial miracle. The kingdom of heaven came to earth, and God's abundance replaced lack. This battle was over.

Strength for the Battle

I'm sure you've experienced the normal battles like car breakdowns and struggles that aren't resolved overnight. Maybe you've had traumatic battles like Shannon's accident or emotional trauma like moving away from family. Just because there's a battle in your life doesn't mean that you aren't pleasing God and doing His will. Quite the opposite is probably the case.

Similarly, many in the Bible walked through trials before they found breakthroughs. Ruth suffered the grief of losing her husband and the difficulty of coming to a brand-new land before she finally entered the season of favor and blessing with Boaz. Esther called for a three-day fast as she planned to daringly risk her life to save the Jews. God honored her steps of boldness and gave her favor with the king. Her great courage brought defeat on Haman and delivered the Jewish people.

Likewise, each new trial presents us with a choice. We can either believe God will bring us through, or we can worry and fret. Psalm 34:19 says, "Many are the afflictions of the righteous, But the Lord delivers him out of them all." He truly is our Deliverer in every situation. And I love that David uses the word *all* because God is able to bring victory without exception.

But it's during those times of battle that faith and maturity grows. People learn patience by trusting God through the storms of life. Hebrews says, "that you do not become sluggish, but imitate those who through faith and patience inherit the promises" (Heb 6:12). Some battles are won in an instant by the authority and power of Jesus Christ, but there is value in the long conflicts. Sometimes the victory is more glorious after a difficult struggle. And through the eyes of expectancy, God provides vision of the hope that is to come.

In Bill Johnson's devotional book *A Life of Miracles*, he says, "Suffering referred to in the Bible means living between two conflicting realities and trusting and praising God through it all."[v]

More Good Was Coming out of Redding

By now, the cute, dark-haired boy, Graham, was steadily dating Candace. Often, he showed up at the front door all dressed up with a bouquet of flowers in his hands. Sometimes he brought flowers for me too, knowing just how to win over the mother's heart. Candace had waited a long time for a good man, and it was becoming obvious that they were made for each other. One day she said to me, "Mom, if we hadn't moved to Redding, I never would have met Graham." The apostle Paul is right; "all things work together for good to those who love God, to those who are the called according to His purpose" (Rom. 8:28).

Trials are a part of life and testimonies come out of tests. So often after intense battles, God helps us wave the flag of victory. The greatest challenge comes right in the heat of the struggle. It often appears that victory will never come, and breakthrough seems impossible. That's when the enemy urges us to wave the flag of surrender and defeat. When our emotions speak louder than the truth of God's Word, it's time to stand and not falter. Paul says, "Stand therefore, having girded your waist with truth ..." (Eph. 6:14). God will bring you to the other side of your difficulty. Meanwhile, He calls you and me to stay in the eye of the storm where there is peace and calm.

Another Battle

But even though God had proven faithful to release joy in my life after I was obedient to move to Redding, our family was about to face an even more difficult challenge. This next one caught me completely off guard.

Our family and new grandson, Judah

Chapter Nine

When You Don't Get What You Expected

Surrendering to the Father

It was January. Much of our family now taught at the private school. The quiet campus was decorated with oak trees and nestled against some small hills. Often, when I drove into the parking lot in the morning, I took a deep breath and feasted my eyes on the beauty and serenity of the school grounds before unloading my car. Candace assisted in the preschool department. Often I would see her leading a trail of tiny tots to the playground like a mother duck with ducklings following in single file. I could hear their squealing, high-pitched voices in the distance. Shannon, in her second year of teaching, was finding favor and enjoyment with the junior high kids. Some days I joined her for lunch in her crowded classroom. Kids pressed in around her desk trying to get as close as possible, hanging on her every word.

That fall I began a string program in the music department. The Lord brought some advanced players to the school, two from China. Teaching strings brought me much more fulfillment than directing bands had in the past. It was Mike's fifth year as the site-principal, and the school was growing. Everything seemed to be going so well. But the unexpected was about to happen.

In order to protect people's identity and honor, I resist giving a detailed account of the events that followed. Suffice it to say that Mike and I love revival, and an anointing of healing visited the campus one day. Not long after, Mike left the school.

Since much of our family worked at the school, we were thrown into a whirlwind of uncertainty. The situation felt like a bad dream, but early on, we chose to forgive. It was a daily decision. Mike and I spent hours in the prayer chapel at church, worshiping, praying, and soaking in the presence of God. Through the conflicting emotions, we anticipated that God was up to something good.

Several months before, Mike had a vivid dream that had alerted us to some potential drastic change in the future. In the dream Mike was walking high on a narrow ledge. It was so narrow that he could easily fall on either side. He walked ten feet, and much to his surprise, there was a drop off where he suddenly walked right off the edge. He plunged down in compete darkness thinking he was going to die. He noticed stars twinkling all around him as he continued to fall. Suddenly, he landed in a fish hatchery. Light replaced darkness, and fish were swimming all around him. At the time of the dream, we felt perplexed at what might happen in Mike's future to make him feel like he was walking off a cliff. Now we knew. But fortunately the dream had a good ending. He landed feet-first in a fish hatchery. Since a fish hatchery is a place that offers protection for small fish to grow and develop before they are thrown into lakes and rivers, we anticipated that we would probably be led to some kind of a school or training place for young people.

Now Mike was on the job hunt, but the next several months were filled with extreme peace. In fact, I had never really felt that much peace even on a good day. People from our church promised that they would hold our arms up until the storm had passed. Up to now, we had trouble finding close friends in Redding. But because of this trial, People were calling, texting, and sending cards. A group of friends met together every week simply to support us. We felt continually encouraged.

In many ways, life was good. We now had more family close by, new friends, a church we loved, a beautiful city, but of course—no job.

June rolled around, and Graham asked for Candace's hand in marriage. They set the wedding date for September, three short months away. I thought, *Surely God wouldn't move us away—not now. We have only lived in Redding for five years.*

To be perfectly honest, I think I felt that because we were trying to do the right things and have the right attitude, God would give us what we wanted now.

Soon Mike applied for a good paying job in the school district, and since he knew the superintendent, it looked like a shoo-in. They called him for an interview, and afterward he felt it went well. But surprisingly, Mike didn't get the job. Next he began writing up plans and discussing the possibility of starting a revival high school. Everything pointed in that direction. Even our friends encouraged him to pursue this dream.

Just to cover ourselves, he sent out résumés to private schools and churches all over the country. However, secretly, or maybe not so secretly, we hoped none of them would call.

Dream Trip

Shortly after Candace got engaged, our friends from Switzerland announced, "We really feel that we are to send you to Switzerland for a vacation. We believe it's the Lord. We'll pay for your flight and some hotels, and we know people that would love to host you. You can even minister in our church." I remember sitting dumbfounded, wondering if this was for real. Then she added, "I think you should stay at least three weeks." Mike had always wanted to go to Switzerland. His great-great-grandfather was from the Bern area, and my mom's relatives had origins in the same region. Ten years earlier, a prophetic friend told us that one day we would be going to Switzerland. Was this the time? Now, when we had no job? Were we to go to Europe just several weeks before our daughter's wedding? It seemed crazy but wonderful.

The next day, Mike encountered our neighbor lady who asked how he was doing. He said, "I'm still out of work, but could you watch over our house for us because we're going to Switzerland for three weeks?" She looked at him like he was nuts.

It wasn't like we had a big savings account that we could rely on to carry us long term. Our money would run out in

September. But we both felt peace that God was leading us to make this trip in July, and it was perfect timing.

Upon arriving, we were put up in one of the nicest hotels in Zurich, enjoyed some wonderful meals, and handed keys to a rental car for the next three weeks of travels. Thanks to our friends, we stayed in hotels and homes all over Switzerland and ministered in a church and some home groups. We took trains up the Alps, listened to yodelers, alphorn players, and enjoyed hiking in the mountains colored with wildflowers, passing friendly cows with ringing bells dangling from their necks. We stayed with a husband and wife for six days that lived in a chalet overlooking Lake Brienz and had the time of our lives.

Back to Reality

Finally, the adventure was over, and Candace and Graham picked us up at the airport. She was all bubbly, talking about wedding plans. Graham, with his big smile, grabbed my suitcase and led us to the car. It was good to be home.

Within a few days, a superintendent from a school in the Bay Area emailed Mike. She offered to fly us both down to interview Mike. I looked on the map to see where Fremont was. I spotted it in the south Bay Area, about forty minutes southeast of the San Francisco airport.

My heart began to wrestle with God. *This can't be Your will, God. You give your children their hearts' desires when they seek after You. You know I want to live near my kids. Five years ago, you asked me to leave family and move to Redding, and I obeyed. Fremont is away from everyone.*

Shannon and Rodney invited us out to dinner a week later. We sat across from them at the table when Shannon handed me a small square box with a little giraffe on it. I opened it to find tiny baby slippers. It took me a moment to realize that this was their way of telling us, "We're pregnant." They had been trying to get pregnant for eleven months. Several months earlier they asked us to join with them in faith to believe for a baby. Now, the day that God told us we were moving away was the day Shannon tested positive for her pregnancy. When I looked at my daughter, I felt so many mixed emotions. I was elated that we were finally having a new grandbaby, but I felt like I was about to abandon her at the beginning of her pregnancy.

No amount of my arguing seemed to turn the mind of God. Everything pointed to Fremont. And this time, we weren't taking any kids (or grandkids) with us. Three weeks after Candace's wedding, Mike drove the rental truck pulling the car, and I took up the rear with the van. We were headed to a city we knew little about except that it was one of the most diverse cities in the United States. During the drive south, my mind wandered back to a dream I had a few years earlier. In the dream, a messenger said, "You and Mike are called to be missionaries in the United States."

Tears kept streaming down my cheeks. I had more questions than answers, but I still had anticipation that God was up to something good. I felt confident in my spirit that

God knew my heart's desire better than I. After all, He formed my very being and knew my destiny. Mike and I had told God years ago that we were a coin in His pocket, and He could spend us any way He liked. We knew that obedience was key to living a life of faith. God didn't say we would understand it all. But we did understand that the safest and most fulfilling place to be is following the Lamb wherever He goes (Rev. 14:4b).

At the same time, I felt loss. I had to let go of how I thought God would lead us. This move was a complete surprise, not at all what I expected. By that point in my life, I knew it was important to let myself grieve. But through the grief, I could stay in hope because of what I know about God. Just because He didn't lead me the way I thought didn't mean I needed to lose confidence that He was holding my future in His loving, trusting hands.

Feeling the mixed emotions, I was reminded of something Heidi Baker told our church several years earlier—that we could expect to drink both the cup of joy and suffering.[vi] That was it. I felt the suffering, but the joy was still there deep down inside. I felt the pleasure of God in my obedience to say yes to Him. "Yes God, I'll go." I could trust in His goodness. This was not the end of my story. I could still anticipate that in the scheme of things, Fremont would ultimately prove to be the best choice. I was blessed to be transitioning with a warm and loving husband. We were doing this together. Several people had already prophesied to us that this was going to be a time of adventure. I hoped with all my heart that one of our adventures would be to see revival come to our new school campus.

Once we were moved into our new home in Fremont, I got out my guitar and began singing the song I wrote a few months earlier back in Redding. Right after Mike left the school and we faced uncertainty, I sat before the Lord in my living room, and the words to this song came to me:

> I live this day with You
> I live one day at a time
> And right now I'm spending time with You
> I'm so in love with You
> You draw me to Your heart
> You whisper words that fill me with new life …
> Chorus: And I can feel Your presence in this place
> All I can see is Your face right in front of me
> In all Your beauty, and all of Your glory …

I sang this song every day for several weeks, and the Spirit of the Lord brought me comfort, peace, and encouragement.

Four Months Later

Four months later, I felt Mike shake me awake at six thirty in the morning. "What is it?" I asked, feeling startled. "It's Jason. Chelsea tried to text me at three o'clock this morning to say that she took him to ER." By now I was sitting upright in bed with my heart pounding thinking about our son. Mike continued, "Chelsea got up in the middle of the night and saw Jason pacing in the living room. When she got closer, she noticed his eyes roll back into his head as he started to pass out. She quickly called 911 and got him to the hospital where they have been trying to figure out what's wrong." I grabbed my glasses on my nightstand and ran to my cell phone. Sure enough, Chelsea had texted me too, but our phones were off.

One hour later, I received a phone message that said, "Pray! Pray! Pray! His spleen has just ruptured!" I ran to tell Mike. Neither of us knew what the function of the spleen was. Was it life threatening? We didn't know. I called my parents. Mom said, "Your cousin had a ruptured spleen, and he seems to be doing fine." I felt a little relief.

Jason, our oldest, married his childhood sweetheart, Chelsea, now a registered nurse. When he was about four years old, he and Chelsea played together while Mike and I led home groups with her parents. At their young ages, the kids both told their mothers separately that they were going to get married someday. But they never voiced that to each other. Sure enough, years later, they met up again at a cousin's wedding and fell in love. Now in 2013, they were living in West Salem with their beautiful daughter, Ella.

Two days earlier they had contacted us to say that they felt a stirring in their hearts that God was up to something new and fresh. There was an excitement in their voices, but Chelsea added, "Pray for Jason. He's had a fever and sore throat that doesn't seem to go away. And he's been unusually tired."

Now we had just received this shocking text message that Jason's spleen had ruptured. Mike and I rallied the troops to pray, called intercessors, and posted requests on Facebook. Minutes later, Chelsea told us that Jason tested positive for mono and that the mono had triggered the rupture. The next few days challenged our emotions. At times his vitals seemed a little more stable, but in an instant they would become erratic—fever and heart rate soaring up. It seemed he was the worst at around three o'clock in the morning. We prayed night and day, trusting God to bring stability and even save his spleen. Chelsea stayed by his side constantly, even setting up a bed next to his. We received updated messages from her every couple of hours.

The whole ordeal reminded me of Shannon's bike accident right after we moved to Redding. I felt the same helplessness, living so far away, but standing on the Word.

My mind traveled back to Sunday at church right before the service started. One of the prayer servants walked up to me and whispered in my ear. "The Lord is giving me a word for you, Cindy. The word is *expectancy.*" Immediately I thought that God was just speaking to me about the theme in this book. But when Jason's life-threatening emergency struck, I knew the word was to encourage me to stay expectant for my son's healing. I think that God in His mercy knew that I was still struggling with all the changes in my life, and to make things a little easier, He gave me one word. It was the word I hung on to for the next several days.

Sure enough, God was true to that revelatory word. Jason was released from the hospital in five days with his spleen intact. Mike and I drove up to Oregon to see him the day after he came home from the hospital.

Two weeks later, Chelsea texted us and asked if Jason could fly down and spend some R & R at our house. He booked plane tickets for a one-week stay. I got to play nursemaid to our thirty-one-year-old son, make meals for him, watch movies together, and drive him to all my favorite palm trees in the area. Jason is the only one in the family that loves palm trees more than me. I kept thanking God for His healing over Jason and for this time of family connection.

Years ago, doctors had said I would never be able to have children, but in 1981 the cycle of barrenness was broken off of me. Then when the kids were old enough to be on their own, God moved us away from them. But God was proving to me that He could keep relationships strong even at a distance. That's just the kind of God He is.

Building Character While You Wait

Have you ever expected God to do something and it didn't work out the way you imagined? Dashed expectations can be as simple as having a friend cancel a coffee date. One person in the Bible that probably expected to see an easier pathway to his destiny was David. After Samuel anointed him to be king, the opposition began. The journey to the throne was paved with years of persecution and pain. But through it all, he let God develop his character. When God leads us down a road we don't expect, we can be assured of one thing; it is part of His plan to prepare us for our destiny. He wants us to fulfill our destiny even more than we do. He can use the pathway, however long it may seem, to build our character and develop the gifts He has placed within us. Surrender is a beautiful thing.

In Scripture, God seems to omit a lot of the emotion that I'm sure biblical characters experienced as they faced difficulty. For example, don't you think Joseph probably felt extremely disappointed when Potiphar's wife wrongfully accused him of immoral behavior and no one came to his rescue? He ended up in jail. Likely, he expected God to come and defend and rescue him right then and there. After all, he had already been betrayed by his brothers and sold into slavery. He was away from his family, living in a foreign land, and adjusting to an unfamiliar culture. Wasn't that trial enough? But it's obvious by the story that Joseph didn't get bitter toward God. He allowed Him to continue to mold and train him for the promotion that lay ahead. He didn't stop expecting God's goodness in his life just because he encountered a detour. He used his God-given gifts and leadership abilities in the prison no differently than he did outside the prison.

Joseph's story was written to encourage God's people of all time. It's a story of endurance. And it reminds us that God is not finished with any of us yet.

If you are faced with some dashed expectations, don't let those experiences paint the picture of your whole life. It's not over. Your final chapter isn't written. God knows the pathway to your destiny. If you feel you're in a prison like Joseph, let your obedience and praises begin to open the gates of freedom. Encourage yourself in the Lord. I'm sure Joseph held fast to the revelatory dreams God gave him years earlier. Cling to all you know about the character of who God is.

Maybe, like David, you have been anointed for a certain task, but you lack any real opportunity to use your gift right now; nothing looks like what you expected. God promised that He would use you in a certain area, but you see no prospect of that happening. You can believe that like David, at the right moment, God will open the door for you.

David says in the Psalms, "Blessed be the Lord God, the God of Israel, Who only does wondrous things!" (Ps. 72:18). He will fulfill the promises He made to you. As long as you have life and breath, you can expect God to work everything out for good (Rom. 8:28). He is building and forming you to be able to handle your future. He knows if He releases any of us into our destiny prematurely, we could crash and burn. Preparation and planting times are just as significant as harvest season. We can't have one without the other. And He's a timing God. Just at the perfect moment, He releases His people into breakthrough and destiny. It may seem like He's forgotten you, but the truth is you are continually on His mind.

Let go of the discouragements of the past so God can bring you into the new. Isaiah 43:18 says, "Do not remember the former things, Nor consider the things of old."

Then he adds, "Behold I will do a new thing, Now it shall spring forth; Shall you not know it? I will even make a road in the wilderness And rivers in the desert" (Isa. 43:19).

It's time to praise Him. Praise Him ahead of time for what He's going to do!

Chapter Ten

The Fuel for Expectancy

Intimacy

I n the previous chapters, I've taken you on a journey through many life experiences. My hope is that you have been inspired to use the tools from Scripture mentioned throughout this book to build yourself up in the faith. God has given us things that we can do to stay encouraged. But all these tools need to be coupled with one important ingredient. It's important to stay thankful, worship, read Scripture, stand on the promises, and keep your mind renewed, but these must be energized by one thing—intimacy with Papa God. It's intimacy with Him and a life of hearing God that continually fuels expectancy.

Friendship with our Father in heaven is the propellant that empowers everything else. This most basic ingredient provides the stamina to actively resist disillusionment and defeat. It enables us to hear the voice of the Lord as we draw close, open our hearts to listen, and enter into His throne room. It's in this place of oneness and presence that He speaks and pours out direction, comfort, correction, and encouragement. Out of His presence we are led by His spirit to be thankful, give Him praise, open the Word, and step out in obedience. These tools help us stay in faith, but there is no formula for relationship. The apostle Paul said, "that I may know Him and the power of His resurrection, and the fellowship of His sufferings ..." (Phil. 3:10). Knowing the Lord and how He relates to us personally keeps us going strong. Relationship with Him fuels the ability to enjoy life and believe that He wants to do extraordinary things for His kids.

There are no shortcuts to developing intimacy with the Father. It's about walking with Him one day at a time, one moment at a time. In this deep place, He gives the strength to stand firm in hardship and hold on to the Rock until breakthrough comes. Often He speaks a revelatory Word that gives the strategy to overcome the enemy. He desires that we see victory even more than we do. And He doesn't just want to meet our needs; He wants to give us all things to enjoy (1 Tim. 6:17).

Sometimes His encouragement is subtle. If you're one that enjoys nature like I do, you can probably remember countless times you happened to step outside just at the right moment only to be captivated by the most beautiful sunrise or sunset. It was as if God hand painted the sky just for you. Or maybe during a certain day you kept encountering people that showed you extraordinary kindness, and you felt the compassion of the Lord coming through their eyes. The simplicity of God's goodness can take on many faces. He uses so many creative ways to connect with His children. And since the Holy Spirit lives in us, He's never far away.

Hearing God

For us to stay strengthened, encouraged, and protected in the Lord, we must be able to hear the voice of God. The Lord says in Hebrews, "I will put My laws in their mind and write them on their hearts; and I will be their God, and they shall be My people. None of them shall teach his neighbor, and none his brother, saying, 'Know the Lord,' for all shall know Me, from the least of them to the greatest of them" (Heb. 8:10b-11). Under the new covenant of God's grace, the Holy Spirit lives in His people and desires to commune with them on a regular basis. But God spoke to, guided, and encouraged those in the Old Testament as well.

I love Nehemiah's story. In the process of rebuilding the walls of Jerusalem, he faced lots of opposition and intimidation. Finally, when Nehemiah's enemies falsely accused him, he prayed to God for strength and wisdom. It was then that Nehemiah *perceived* from God that there was a plot against his life (Neh. 6:12-13). Because of the discernment that God gave him, the walls were completed in such a way that even his enemies knew he was assisted by God.

The same is true in our lives. When our ears are open to God's voice, He gives strategies and encouragement to overcome life's obstacles and stay close to His heart.

Obedience

At times God gives words of correction just like a father would correct a son that runs out into a busy street. When the son listens and runs back into the arms of the father, he returns to the canopy of protection. It's here in the place of obedience to the voice of God that the believer can expect to live out a life of hope. It's under this cloak of protection that we will hear the encouraging words of the Father. And His world intersects with our world continually since He is forever communicating with His sons and daughters. But if we're not listening or staying under His protection, we can miss much of what He's trying to say. And if we don't hear His voice, we can't act upon it.

It's interesting that Abraham was called a *friend of God* because his works (obedience) coincided with his faith when he offered up his son on the altar. This act of obedience pleased God. It's not enough to simply have a belief system; our works need to be combined with our faith.

How Does He Speak?

If you've known God for any length of time, you've probably been pursued by Him in many different ways. He knows how to captivate our hearts in a way that stirs up a hunger on the inside of us. It leaves us with a longing for more of His presence. We were created to have deep fellowship with Him. Sometimes His voice is clear and immediately resonates with our spirits. Other times, it seems we have to search high and low for Him. It's almost as if He hides Himself, but He doesn't hide so well that He can't be found. The Lord says, "And you will seek Me and find Me, when you search for Me with all your heart. I will be found by you, says the Lord ..." (Jer. 29:13-14). Life with God is an adventure of conversations and exchanges going back and forth.

Have you ever awakened in the morning with a song in your head? You start singing the words, and oddly enough, they are exactly what you need to hear that morning? Or maybe you had a refreshing dream in the night, and you know in your heart that it's a message from God. The images are so vivid; you think about it all day long. What about the times you've attended church and the teaching from the pastor stirs up your faith? You leave feeling revived. Or maybe you opened your Bible and a verse leaped off the page, offering complete peace to your tormented soul. You found inspiration to trust God once again. There are so many ways that God speaks and encourages His children. He's always attempting to communicate with us. It's a matter of us being tuned in to His frequency and receiving the message. Sometimes He speaks in such subtle whispers that the words or ideas can be barely heard. Just like in human relationships, it's important for us to be good listeners. It's far easier to do all the talking.

The Father loves to give His people revelation that they can hold on to throughout the difficult seasons. Just one word from Him can keep us anticipating His goodness. So we can daily expect to receive just the right encouragement from Him. The following list is by no means exhaustive but contains some valuable ways God communicates with His people.

The Written Word

I believe that one of the primary ways that God speaks to His children is through the inspired Scriptures. When we invite the Holy Spirit to breathe life into us through the words on the page, we can expect to eat of His fresh manna. Day after day He desires to feed us something new. It's not a religious exercise but a communion between a father and a son or daughter. Surprisingly, verses we have read hundreds of times can take on new meaning. In the written Word, we can spend a lifetime getting to know more of God's nature and ways. But along with getting to know who God is, we often receive direct and practical messages for our current life experiences.

The pages of the Bible are charged with promises of hope, and the more we apply His words to our lives, the more we're able to stand firm in the heat of the battle. In Proverbs, it says, "My son, give attention to my words; Incline your ear to my sayings. Do not let them depart from your eyes; Keep them in the midst of your heart; For they are life to those who find them, And health to all their flesh" (Prov. 4:20–22). The very words of God bring us life and health.

Over the years, I've memorized many Bible promises that have been a lifeline for me more times than I can count. When I declare them out loud, the truth gets into my spirit, my faith is rejuvenated, and the power of those living words scares the enemy away. That's how Jesus defeated satan in the wilderness. He spoke out Scripture and the devil eventually left him alone (Matt. 4).

Dreams: A Message in the Night

In the body of Christ, there has been little emphasis placed on the importance of dreams or dream interpretation. But more and more I see a resurgence of interest and anointing for this form of God-communication. Since God spoke to mankind through dreams in the Bible, we can trust that He still does so today. As I quoted earlier, Hebrews says, "Jesus Christ is the same yesterday, today, and forever" (Heb. 13:8). And through these mysteries in the night seasons, He often sheds light on our human relationships and reveals our own hearts. Other times, He gives keys that can help us connect more deeply with the Father. Sometimes He sounds a warning to protect us from unknown danger.

In 1996, I began having dreams on a regular basis. Since I knew in my spirit that they had significant meaning, I wrote them all down in my journal. But I had no idea what any of them meant. Four years later, I met a prophetic woman who helped me interpret some of them, and soon a whole new world of learning and hearing God began to open up to me. When I studied Scripture, I noticed that many people received messages from God through dreams or visions.

In my journey with God, He has often given me a preview of an event to come through a dream. Four years before I actually moved to Fremont, I had a dream that Mike and I moved south to the San Francisco Bay Area. However, when I had the dream, I assumed that it was symbolic, not literal. Later, when we were offered the job in the Bay Area, the dream became another confirmation that this was the direction that God was leading us.

God can use a message in a dream to keep a person encouraged even before he faces a trial. Early in his life, Joseph had dreams of greatness. Later, when evil started to attack him, no doubt he hung on for dear life to the promises in those two dreams. He persevered through severe trials before he saw the long awaited fulfillment. Throughout the Bible, people were often given encouragement before they encountered trouble.

One night I had a dream. I was playing soccer with some of my husband's soccer friends from college. My eyes noticed their strong biceps and calf muscles. Suddenly, an opposing player kicked the ball to me. I tried to connect with it and give it a good kick, but my leg wouldn't move. It was extremely weak and limp. I tried again and this time successfully kicked the ball.

I woke up asking the Holy Spirit what the dream could mean. I wasn't aware of any unusual weakness to my body at the time. So I simply put the dream away.

Months later, I dreamed that I was a passenger on a train walking down the aisle looking for my strong son. Finally at the back of the train I found him and noticed his powerful arm muscles. I embraced him and then woke up. I had no idea what these two dreams meant until later when the doctor diagnosed me with severe chronic fatigue. Because of these dreams and other revelation from God, I knew I was going to be strong and have energy again. I hung on to what I knew the Lord showed me ahead of time. Sure enough, eventually I was completely healed.

In dreams, God often uses pictures, symbols, and parables to relay a message. In his book *The Illustrated Bible-Based*

Dictionary of Dream Symbols, Dr. Joe Ibojie says, "Those who have understood the tremendous power of symbols have gained incredible insight into the mysteries of God, because God's ways are wrapped up in the language of symbolism."[vii] My husband is an athlete, and his dreams are filled with sporting events like soccer and football games. Since I'm a musician, God often uses music symbols to describe the details of my life.

One night, in a dream, I saw two pages of music. I noticed that the piece of music started out in one key, but the second page had a key change. When I woke up, I knew that God was saying I could expect a *key change* in my life soon.

Sometimes, when I ask people if they remember their nighttime dreams, they respond by saying, "My dreams are all weird. They can't mean anything." But I remind them that the Egyptian pharaoh's dream about the seven skinny cows eating the seven fat cows was pretty weird (Gen. 41). And it's amazing to me that the pharaoh's spirit was so troubled after the dream that he sent for all the magicians and all the wise men of Egypt to help him interpret its meaning. That's pretty interesting that a person that didn't know God was aware that his dream was significant. And it's even more surprising that the pharaoh was convinced that Joseph's interpretation was correct.

When we ask God for direction or encouragement in our lives, we don't choose how it's going to come. He may give us a dream like He did for so many in the Old and New Testaments. In the life of Jesus' earthly father, Joseph, an angel of the Lord appeared to him in a dream and told him to take Mary as his wife (Matt. 1:20). That dream changed the whole outcome of the story.

One unknown person said that "a dream uninterpreted is like a letter unopened." Proverbs says, "It is the glory of God to conceal a matter, But the glory of kings is to search out a matter" (Prov. 25:2). The Holy Spirit is the one who is able to interpret the message God is giving. So we must search out the matter with the help of the Spirit of the Lord.

I think one of the biggest obstacles that people face when it comes to dreams is that even if they remember them upon awakening, within a few seconds they can be easily forgotten. So it's helpful to place a pad and pen or tape recorder by the bedside to immediately record what you remember. That's exactly what Daniel did when he wrote down his dream and told the main facts in Daniel 7.

There are many different types of dreams. Some dreams reveal the emotion that the dreamer is experiencing at the time. Other dreams can be prophetic or a warning type of dream. However, some dreams are false. If a dream contains a message that contradicts Scripture, or tells you to do something that isn't biblical, it's not from God because no dream from God departs from the truth of Scripture.

As was implied earlier, most dreams are not literal but figurative, like parables or riddles. Reading the parables in the gospels and the symbols in the Book of Revelation can help with dream interpretation. If you have no idea what a certain symbol might represent, it can be helpful to search the dictionary or concordance for a clue.[viii] Also, pay attention to your feelings or thoughts in the dream; these may contain a message. There are many good books on this subject written by reliable Christian authors. But they are quick to emphasize that it's important to get confirmation from the Holy Spirit. Before anything else, it is vital to pray and seek direction and interpretation from the Spirit of God. It is He that gives the ultimate peace about the message because, as I mentioned before, life with God is about relationship, not formula. And just like Joseph said to the pharaoh when asked if he was able to interpret dreams, "It is not in me; God will give Pharaoh an answer of peace" (Gen. 41:16).

Visions

There's little difference between dreams and visions. One occurs during the night and one more often during the day. However, a person could have a vision during the night or a dream during the day (Job 33:14–18).

In Peter's sermon in Acts 2, he shares three ways that God speaks to His children. One is dreams, another is visions, and the third is prophecy. These are signs of the last days as God pours out His spirit.

> "And it shall come to pass afterward
> That I will pour out My Spirit on all flesh;
> Your sons and your daughters shall prophesy,
> Your old men shall dream dreams,
> Your young men shall see visions."—Joel 2:28

There are different types of visions. Rick Joyner says that some come as impressions on the mind. Others come on the conscious level, and some are open visions and viewed "with the clarity of a movie screen."ix Also, people in the Bible like Peter and Paul experienced trances. Joyner goes on to say, "Trances are like dreaming when you're awake."x

For years I assumed that those who received visions were always seeing pictures clearly, like watching a movie screen. It wasn't until a friend taught me that visions and prophetic words can come as impressions through the spiritual senses. Our spirits have eyes, ears, and noses and so forth. We can see, hear, touch, and smell in the spirit realm. That's what Paul meant when he prayed that "the eyes of your understanding [would be] enlightened" (Eph. 1:18). The eyes of the heart are the spiritual eyes, not the physical ones.

Of course there are counterfeits to all the gifts. There are false prophesies, dreams, and visions just like there are false teachers. But there can't be a counterfeit if there is no genuine article. Just because people misuse a gift doesn't mean it should be done away with altogether. It's important to exercise discernment when it comes to all the gifts of the Holy Spirit. Pay attention to the check in your spirit.

I think one of the greatest contaminates to spiritual gifts, hearing God, and intimacy in general is unforgiveness or bitterness. If a person gives a prophecy, teaching, or relays a vision but holds on to unforgiveness, the message becomes contaminated. Bitterness blocks the communication line between us and God. God wants to purify hearts so that the underlying motive in both ministry and relationship is love.

Prophecy

Next, Paul emphasizes the importance of the gift of prophecy in 1 Corinthians when he says, "Pursue love, and desire spiritual gifts, but especially that you may prophesy" (I Cor. 14:1). Basic prophecy is encouragement, edification, and comfort. Paul tells us to desire to prophesy because "he who prophesies speaks edification and exhortation and comfort to men" (1 Cor. 14:3). Most of the time, when people have given me a prophetic word, it has been a confirmation of something that God already told me in my relationship with Him. It confirms that I am hearing God's voice and growing in intimacy. But there have been times that I have received brand-new information. At that point, I asked the Lord, *Is this message from You?* When a prophetic friend prophesied that we were going to Switzerland someday, this word birthed in me a love for the nations that I didn't have before. The prophetic word stirred expectation in my heart for something I had never experienced and would never have thought possible. And when the choice came to actually go to Switzerland, I knew in my heart that it was the Lord confirming the prophetic word that we received years ago.

Some prophetic words I've been given I believe were from God, but I'm still waiting for Him to bring them to pass. I'm hanging on to them by faith. The apostle Paul charged Timothy to wage warfare regarding the prophecies that were made concerning him (I Tim. 1:18). Sometimes we need to believe for and grab hold of revelatory words that have been spoken over our lives.

Later Paul says, "I wish you all spoke with tongues, but even more that you prophesied . . . that the church may receive edification" (1 Cor. 14:5). *Webster's Dictionary* says that to edify means "to instruct in such a way as to improve, enlighten, or uplift morally or spiritually."[xi] Prophecy is another way that God speaks in order to build up the body of Christ.

See the Recommended Reading section for a list of books that you may find helpful that further explain the gift of prophecy.

Teaching

Most Christians are very familiar with the gift of teaching. Many of us expect to hear God when we listen to our pastors and teachers. We can all probably testify to the times we have been strengthened through a gifted teacher, whether it's a friend or a person in a teaching position.

In the book of Acts, Paul and Barnabas preached to the people of various cities and "[strengthened] the souls of the disciples, exhorting them to continue in the faith, and saying, 'We must through many tribulations enter the kingdom of God'" (Acts 14:22). Later, Paul joins Silas and Timothy to help strengthen the churches (Acts 16:5). The same is true today. Many people exercise the gift of teaching to strengthen others in the body. We can all be encouraged by the teaching of an anointed leader.

Impressions

Sometimes God connects with us by giving an impression about something, and we just know that He's speaking. There's a deep awareness in our spirit. Some call it an inclination. God spoke to Elijah in a still, small voice (1 Kings 19:12). Have you ever been driving down a highway when suddenly you feel impressed to pray for someone? Later, you find out that they were in trouble at that exact instant you prayed. That was the Holy Spirit. It's easy to dismiss those gentle nudges. But the more we're obedient to His still, small voice, the more we will receive those special messages.

God Can Speak through Others

God can use people around us, including our immediate family, to speak a word of encouragement into our hearts. Often we expect a great revelatory word to come from an anointed leader or from a vision but not from someone close to us, even living with us. As we keep our spiritual antennas up, we can regularly receive signals from God even in those day-to-day experiences with people we know and love.

Getting Familiar with His Voice

Some people say, "I don't know if what I'm hearing is really God speaking. Maybe it's just my own thinking." And if we're honest, we've probably all struggled with that question from time to time. But the more we get to know Him, the more we recognize His voice. Just like when my husband calls me on the phone, I know it's him because I know his voice. I can tell by his tone what mood he's in. I've been married to him for thirty-six years, and I've developed a deep trust in him as a person. Similarly, the more we spend time with God, hear His voice, and get to know His character, the more we can expect to hear Him and watch Him lavish His love on us. Again, whatever God says to His people never contradicts what He has already said in His Word. And the more we get the Scripture inside of us, the more we understand the character and ways of God.

My earthly father is a man of his word. As a little girl, I knew that whatever Dad said he would do he did. In fact, my dad was never late. If he said he was coming to my school program, he was the first one there. He possessed God's character quality of dependability and trustworthiness, and his words were always carried out. Even if you weren't privileged to have a dependable dad like me, the more you get to know Abba Father, the more you will trust His Word. He never fails. The Lord promises that "Every good gift and every perfect gift is from above, and comes down from the Father of lights, with whom there is no variation or shadow of turning" (James 1:17). He is an unchanging, unwavering God, and His Word is the same.

Learning to Rest

In order to receive more downloads from the Holy Spirit and go deeper in relationship with God, we need to position ourselves in a place of rest. Hebrews says, "There remains therefore a rest for the people of God. For he who has entered His rest has himself also ceased from his works as God did from His" (Heb. 4:9-10). As Christians, most of us understand that we can't produce our salvation through good works, but many of us have difficulty staying in peace after we're saved. God has had me in training over the past few years to learn to do things out of rest. I'm still learning, but I can quickly recognize when I've stepped out of peace.

I remember when I was diagnosed with chronic fatigue in 2009. In the beginning, my adrenal glands were completely shot. I felt disappointed that I didn't have the energy to contribute anything to God. I didn't even have the strength to get out my guitar and worship Him.

One day I voiced that frustration to Him and waited for His response. He told me clearly, *Your rest is worship to Me.* Those words changed my life. A level of striving fell off of me that day.

When we stay in peace and trust, it's easier to connect with and receive from God. There's a new element of security in our relationship. God isn't looking for sloppy, disobedient followers. He desires hearts that have learned dependence on the Father and confidence that He will do what He says He will do. When we rest in God, we are ultimately saying that the breakthrough is not going to happen because of our capability or our human strength, but it's going to happen because our God is mighty and able to save.

We've all heard about women who try for years to get pregnant with no success. Then right after they sign adoption papers, they conceive a child. Worry, struggle, and strife do not contribute to the conception process. Our efforts do not bring us salvation, and our trying does not bring healing. Our rest and dependence upon the Savior opens the door for our High Priest to help us in our time of need (Heb. 4:16).

Resting is not being lazy. I find it interesting that Hebrews 4:11 says, "Let us therefore be diligent to enter that rest...." *Webster's Dictionary* says that the word *diligent* means "persevering and careful in work; industrious."[xii] It almost seems like an oxymoron to use the word *diligence* with the word *rest*. But if we worry or are overproductive, we walk away from that place of childlike dependency on the Holy Spirit. When we walk in the Spirit, we are branches that stay connected to the life-giving source, the Vine. Then we are able to glorify the Father and bear fruit in the kingdom (John 15:7-8). Also we can more easily receive from Him all that He wants to generate to us.

I believe that God is searching for people to be a habitation of His presence. If we can continue to operate out of rest, He can more easily find a home in our hearts. Moses said in Exodus, "If Your presence does not go with us, do not bring us up from here" (Ex. 33:15b). Trying to live out the Christian life without the presence is ineffective. There will always be temptations to let our lives become cluttered, but seeking to operate out of rest will produce far more for the kingdom. We can be carriers of the Holy Spirit wherever we are. There's nothing more satisfying in all of life than to be saturated in His presence. The more we hang out with Christ and let Him fill our thirsty souls, the more our longing hearts find deep fulfillment. And it's really only in this place that we can remain consistently in hope and more able to hear God's voice.

Like many of us, Abraham became impatient because God still hadn't fulfilled His promise. So he decided to help God by going into Hagar to try to have the promised son. But the slave mentality is never going to produce the promise. When we strive in the flesh, it always becomes counterproductive to the Spirit. Just like Abraham, fulfillment of the promise comes through the free woman.

The Best for Last

In writing this book, I saved the best for this last chapter. Intimacy and relationship with God fuel the faith-filled life. Without it, we have little more than positive thinking. God is calling His people to come and sit at His feet, eat at His table, anticipate His goodness, and learn to journey with Him. The power to overcome begins here. What a privilege to get closer to the one true living God and become more familiar with His voice. In that place of intimacy and rest, expectancy is born, and God-confidence will carry us through the difficult times. It will sweep us into supernatural breakthroughs. The vision of our assured future inspires us as the realization of God's dependability and love resonates deep in our souls. It doesn't matter what we see in the natural, and it doesn't matter how long it's been. Living a lifestyle of encountering Jesus generates the perseverance that strengthens us until we obtain the promises.

God can awaken us daily to anticipate that the eyes of our hearts will be "enlightened; [that we would] know what is the hope of His calling, what are the riches of the glory of His inheritance in the saints, and what is the exceeding greatness of His power toward us who believe, according to the working of His mighty power . . ." (Eph. 1:18–19).

As I close, I would like to bless you with the following prayer:

Prayer

"I pray that you would behold the glory of the Lord and come to know His wonderful thoughts toward you. Let Him continually fill you with His all-fulfilling presence and refresh and rejuvenate your spirit man to be strong, giving you great courage. I pray that you would enter into His rest, hear His voice, and stay expectant, positioning yourself to receive your promises from heaven and go from victory to victory. I ask that the anointing and great power of Jesus Christ of Nazareth break off bondages, sicknesses, and lack and usher into your life more of His blessed kingdom. And let intimacy with Christ propel you into your entire destiny. For the Lord says:

'I have called you by your name; You are Mine. When you pass through the waters, I will be with you; And through the rivers, they shall not overflow you. When you walk through the fire, you shall not be burned, Nor shall the flame scorch you. For I am the Lord your God, The Holy One of Israel, your Savior'" (Isa. 43:1b–3a).

Endnotes

Preface

i. Crosby, Fanny J. and Phoebe P. Knapp. *Blessed Assurance.* The New Church Hymnal, Lexington Music Inc. 1976, 144.

Chapter 5

ii. Joyner, Rick. *A Prophetic Vision for the 21ˢᵗ Century.* Nashville, TN: Thomas Nelson, Inc. 1999, 59.

Chapter 6

iii. Bill Johnson, spoken in many sermons.

Chapter 7

iv. Kimmel, Elizabeth. *Ladies First: 40 Daring Women Who were Second to None.* Washington, DC: National Geographic Children's Books, 2006, 106–109.

Chapter 8

v. Johnson, Bill. *A Life of Miracles.* Shippensburg, PA: Destiny Image Publishers, Inc., 2009, Day 104.

Chapter 9

vi. Baker, Heidi. "A Cup of Suffering and Joy." Iris Ministries Canada, April 4, 2007, www.http://irismin.ca/news/cup-suffering-and-joy.

Chapter 10

vii. Ibojie, Joe, MD. *The Illustrated Bible-Based Dictionary of Dream Symbols.* San Giovanni Teatino (CH), Italy: Destiny Image Europe, 2005, 9.

viii. Parrott, Joy. *Parables in the Night Seasons, Understanding Your Dreams.* Renton, WA: Glory Publications, 2002, 110.

ix. Joyner, Rick. *The Final Quest.* New Kensington, PA: Whitaker House, 1996, 10.

x. Ibid., 11.

xi. *Webster*'s *New World Dictionary of American English, Third College Edition.* New York, NY: Simon & Schuster, Inc. 1972.

xii. *Webster's New World Dictionary of American English, Third College Edition.* New York, NY: Simon & Schuster, Inc. 1972.

Recommended Reading

Books on Prophesy

Developing Your Prophetic Gifting by Graham Cooke
The Beginner's Guide to the Gift of Prophesy by Jack Deere

Books on Intimacy and Relationship with God

Face to Face with God by Bill Johnson
Strengthen Yourself in The Lord by Bill Johnson

Books on Dreams and Dream Interpretation

Understanding the Dreams You Dream by Ira Milligan
*The Illustrated Bible-Based Dictionary of
Dream Symbols* by Dr. Joe Ibojie
Interpreting the Symbols and Types by Kevin J. Conner

Books on Healing

When Heaven Invades Earth by Bill Johnson
Smith Wigglesworth: The Secret of
His Power by Albert Hibbert
John G. Lake: A Man Without Compromise by Wilford Reidt

For more information

or

to contact Cindy Wenger
for a speaking engagement

Email her at: mcwenger@att.net
Or log on to her Website at: www.livinginexpectancy.com